Alchemy

Of

Ayurvedic Cookery

Cover and book design by PranaJi.com

Cover photography © Jakub Gojda

Alchemy of Ayurvedic Cookery

July 2016.

Alchemy of Ayurvedic Cookery

Shazia Gogia

ShazYogaAyurveda.com

When diet and lifestyle is *inappropriate*, medicinals are of no use. When diet and lifestyle is *appropriate*, medicinals are of no need.

~ Ayurvedic proverb

Table of Contents

III

IV

About the Author

Shazia Gogia is a Yoga Teacher, Integrative Yoga Therapist, Ayurvedic Practitioner and Ayuredic Chef. She has a BS, MBA, E-RYT500 (Experienced Registered Yoga Teacher with Yoga Alliance) and more than 1000 hours in Ayurvedic medicine.

Shazia eats only plant-based diet and follows principles of Ayurveda in her teachings, cooking, healing in order to live a healthier and happier life. As an Ayurvedic Practitioner and Chef, she works one-on-one with "your" unique constitution, life style, challenges, health issues, constraints and constitutional pattern of body-mind-consciousness. Shazia also teaches Hatha yoga, therapeutic yoga and meditation. She teaches workshops and teachers trainings in yoga, Ayurveda and Ayurvedic cooking locally and internationally.

Shazia became vegetarian when she married her husband, Prana Gogia. She considers Prana as her real teacher and attributes most of her life transformation to his teachings, wisdom, kindness, patience, and gifted hands. Prana is Doctor of Acupuncture and Oriental Medicine, Licensed Acupuncturist, Herbalist and teacher of Ayurveda and CranioSacral Work.

Shazia treats food as medicine, her body as a temple, lives mindfully, and teaches with awareness and unconditional love. She has healed herself from many physical issues and attributes her healing to Ayurveda, yoga, meditation, attitude, happy heart, and a great zest for life.

Shazia lives with her husband, Prana Gogia in sunny San Diego, California.

Shazia's Website: shazyogaayurveda.com

Shazia's Facebook: facebook.com/shaziagogia

Shazyogaayurveda on Facebook:
facebook.com/shazyogaayurveda

Prana on Facebook: facebook.com/dr.pranaji

Prana's website: PranaJiAcupuncture.com

Acknowledgements

My sister Nazia in Calgary tried most of my recipes. My friend Danielle sowed the seed for writing a book and helped so much in editing.

My friend Zillah came to all my cooking workshops, lent me her two strong hands and lovingly joked that she will publish my recipes if I did not. Tina and Megan edited tirelessly.

My friend Laura Lee made the recipes alive by styling and photographing most of the dishes in this book. I am so thankful to her for her creativity and patience.

My husband Prana, who is a very experienced and wise Ayurvedic Practitioner and Doctor of Acupuncture and Oriental Medicine, has double-checked recipes' effects on three doshas. Since he has taught me to cook Indian vegetarian food many years ago, he is the force behind my cooking. He also did all publishing and formatting.

I thank all of them with a sincere heart for all their efforts, for pushing me, for believing I could do this, and so happy that they played along.

Shazia Gogia,

July 2016, San Diego, CA.

Introduction

"Alchemy of Ayurvedic Cookery" was birthed from a deep love of cooking, eating, and sharing of food. I love the exploration that food allows me, flavors, textures, bounty of fresh and juicy vegetables, aromas, trying new foods and dishes. I rarely follow recipes. Creating delicious food is a trade of the heart. I try something new and mold it and shape it until it tastes delicious. Since most of my dishes are new each time I make them, writing a book that requires exact measurements was a challenge. It was also a great learning experience.

I became a vegetarian when I married my wonderful husband, a wise decision that changed my life forever. My mother taught me how to cook, but it was my husband who "really" taught me how to cook: beautiful layering of spices, the order of things, how to balance cooling or heating vegetables with certain spices, the health benefits of each spice and the delicacy of Indian spices. He taught me the Ayurvedic principles of food combining as well as how to help bring individuals to balance through food as medicine. My curiosity and tongue took me outside the traditional Indian kitchen and Ayurvedic recipes. I tasted many world cuisines, eventually trying them in my kitchen and then trying to master them. The journey was long and delicious…. And still continues….

All recipes in this book are vegetarian using plant-based foods and based on time-tested principles of Ayurveda. I use a lot of ghee (clarified butter) and milk occasionally for a dessert. Ghee can be easily replaced with any high smoke-point vegetable oil. Coconut milk or Almond milk easily replaces milk.

Not all Indian food that you eat in restaurants is Ayurvedic. My recipes have been adapted to AVOID unhealthy practices like excessive cooking time, very high-heat cooking, deep frying, using pressure cooker, Tarka (frying whole spices in oil or ghee and topping on already cooked lentils and curries), white-flour naan, to name a few…

I live in southern California where nature's bounty is plentiful. I get to try so many cuisines, visit farmers markets throughout the year and eat some of the best and freshest produce in USA. Therefore, I added a whole section on "Healthy Foods and International Recipes" that are balanced Ayurvedically, using nutritionally dense foods, fresh local and seasonal produce, and minimal cooking time. Besides, I cannot eat Indian every day.

How I made Ayurvedic cooking simple and knowing these tips before you start:

- All recipes in this book have an Ayurvedic key at top:

+ means increases

- means decreases

= means no effect

- Ayurveda teaches us to eat according to seasons. I have always considered season's effects, availability of produce and suitability of certain foods in winter versus summer.

- You can start cooking Ayurvedically just with a handful of basic Indian spices. See next page heading "Spices: essentials".

- I grind my own spices but you can buy them in powder form at any Indian or Middle Eastern grocery store. However, always grind your own green cardamom seeds. They can stay potent and aromatic for at least two months in your pantry in an air-tight container if you grind them yourself. Store bought green cardamom powder is already flat and has already lost its aroma.

- Basmati rice DOES NOT have to be pre-soaked.

- Soaking lentils and beans reduces time to cook them and saves on energy bill.

- I use ghee (clarified butter) most frequently. Store-bought is Ok. Ghee's health benefits surpass any other oils. Ghee is considered to be most vital of the dairy medicines. It penetrates deep into tissues, taking herbs and spices along with it into your bodily tissues. Ghee, not only provides nourishment but also confidence, promotes memory and vital bodily essence (ojas).

- Ghee measurements in this book are for melted ghee.

- I do not recommend cooking in olive oil. Olive oil has a very low smoke point. It should be used raw and not for cooking. Instead use ghee (clarified butter) or oils with high smoke point like rice bran oil, avocado oil, and coconut oil.

- I use fresh Indian or Thai green chilies and freshly grounded black pepper for "heat" in my food. I do not like to use any red chilies as they are hard on your stomach lining.

- Some recipes may not include a protein. I always throw in some cooked beans. If beans do not just get along in a particular recipe, I serve a side of spiced beans or some type of tofu or tempeh sauté or freshly baked tofu.

- I use low-sodium tamari and low-sodium soy-sauce. When using either of these two ingredients in recipes, do not add salt until you taste it. You can always add more but cannot remove.

The book is divided into:

- **Traditional Indian Recipes**

- **Sizzling Soups around the World**

- **Healthy Foods and International Recipes balanced Ayurvedically**

- **Middle Eastern (contains more zesty soups)**

- **Sweet Stuff**

What is Ayurveda

Ayurveda, the science of longevity, is a rich traditional medicine of India going back to ancient times. The great seers and sages that produced India's original systems of yoga and meditation also established Ayurveda. Originating as part of Vedic science, Ayurvedic provides a comprehensive view of the entirety of matter, mind, and consciousness.

Adaptable to many different times, cultures and climates, Ayurveda has gone through several stages of development in its long history, spreading east into Indonesia and Indochina as part of Indian culture and west to the Greeks, who developed a similar form of natural medicine. Buddhists brought new insights to Ayurveda and carried it to many different lands with their religion. Ayurveda became the basis of the healing traditions of Tibet, Sri Lanka, and Burma, as well as influencing Chinese medicine. Many great Buddhist sages such as Nagarjuna were Ayurvedic doctors and authors. Today, Ayurveda, in yet another stage of development, is reaching out to the Western world and addressing modern conditions. The medicine of India has much in common with Chinese traditions, allowing it to serve as a point of integration between them. The medicine necessary to heal the planet and usher in a new age of world unity is contained within this, perhaps the oldest of all healing systems.

Doshas: the three constitutional patterns of life-forces

Ayurveda recognizes three primary patterns of life-forces in the body, or doshas, called vata, pitta, and kapha. These dosha correspond to the qualities of motion, transformation, and dynamic-structure. When out of balance, they are the causative forces behind the disease process.

Vata is the biological pattern of movement, also sometimes translated as 'wind'. It is the motivating force behind the other two doshas, which are 'lame', incapable of movement without it. Vata dosha governs sensory and mental balance and orientation and promotes mental adaptability and comprehension.

Pitta is the biological pattern of transformation and metabolism, meaning 'that which digests things'. Pitta dosha is responsible for all transformations in the body. It also governs our mental digestion, our capacity to perceive reality and understand things as they are.

Kapha is the biological pattern of support and fluidity. It provides substance, gives support, and makes up the bulk of our bodily tissues. Kapha dosha also provides our emotional support in life, relating positive emotional traits like love, compassion, modesty, patience and forgiveness.

Here is simple quiz to discover your Ayurvedic Constitution: *pranajiacupuncture.com/prakruti/*

Ayurvedic Cooking

Ayurvedic food is prepared in a way that all six tastes (through herbs and spices) are present in your meal. The food is nourishing not only for the body but also for the mind. Poor combinations of food produce indigestion, fermentation, gas and if pro-longed, can lead to dis-ease. Spices and herbs are added to make foods compatible or to ease the negative effects of foods. Herbs and spices are added not only to enhance the taste of food but also to stimulate the agni (digestive fire), to increase digestion and absorption, and to help counteract any incompatible food combinations.

Your own unique prakruti (constitution) is the map to discovering the foods and lifestyle that will balance you. For example, there is a big misconception that salads are good for everyone. This is not true for Vata (air) dominant person. Similarly, some foods that provide relief in summer may become too cooling for the body in winter. For example, banana and yogurt will lead to mucus and other cold problems for a Kapha dominant person. Eating some dairy at 12pm (when your agni or metabolic fire is high), in the heat of summer may not aggravate Kapha dosha as severely as it would on cold wintry or rainy days. In contrast, eating jalapeno, tomatoes and lemon filled salsa on a hot summer noon OR eggplant, tomatoes and garlic filled Middle-Eastern recipe during heat of summer may drive you crazy if you are predominately Pitta or your pitta is deranged.

I use generous amounts of herbs, numerous spices, turmeric, ginger, garlic, ghee (clarified butter), lemon/lime, and cilantro to balance food. Lentils (dals), legumes and beans, and tofu provide protein for body instead of meat and eggs. Rice (called King of grains) and quinoa provide body with necessary clean carbohydrates. Ghee (clarified butter) considered to be most vital of the dairy medicines penetrates deep into tissues, taking herbs along with it into your bodily tissues. Ghee, not only provides nourishment but also confidence, promotes memory and vital bodily essence (ojas). Instead of using flours, sugar and butter in desserts, mine are made with nuts, chia seeds, hemp seeds, coconut, maple syrup, dried fruits, dates etc.

Shall we head to kitchen now?

Diet Guideline for Three Dosha

	VATA Cold and Dry, Light, Mobile.	**PITTA** Hot and Moist.	**KAPHA** Cold and Damp, Slow, Heavy.
AVOID	Bitter, Astringent, Pungent. Dried fruits. Melons. Raw vegetables & salads. Potato. Ice-cream. Beef.	Sour, Salty, Pungent. Sour fruits (bananas, papayas, tomatoes). Pungent vegetables (garlic). Nuts. Chilies/peppers. Sour cream, cheese, yogurt. Wheat. Pickles. Heat producing vegetables (eggplant).	Sweet, Sour, Salty. Sweet and sour fruits. Sweet and juicy vegetables. Bananas. All Dairy except ghee. Nuts.

	VATA Cold and Dry, Light, Mobile.	PITTA Hot and Moist.	KAPHA Cold and Damp, Slow, Heavy.
FAVOR	Sweet, Sour. Soups/ stews. Cooked, steamed, or sautéed vegetables. Nuts (soaked) Dairy.	Sweet, Bitter, Astringent. Cucumbers. Melons. Oranges. Salads, raw, sprouts.	Pungent, Bitter, Astringent. Apples, berries, all greens.
TO PACIFY	Sweet, Salty, Sour, Spicy. Warming, moistening, nutritive foods. Foods that promote weight. Most spices OK: (ginger, garlic, coriander, cumin, clove,	Bitter, Sweet, Astringent. Cooling / Heat-dispelling foods. Detoxify heat in liver.	Pungent, Bitter, Astringent, Spicy. Warming, drying, heating and stimulating food. Most spices OK: (ginger, garlic, coriander, cumin, clove,

cinnamon, black pepper, green cardamom, allspice, nutmeg). Carminative and purgative and laxative herbs (flaxseed).		cinnamon, black pepper, green cardamom, allspice, nutmeg).

Spices for Three Dosha

VATA	PITTA	KAPHA
Allspice	Basil	Allspice
Asafetida	Black Pepper	Asafetida
Basil	(moderation)	Basil
Bay Leaves	Green	Bay Leaves
Black Pepper	cardamom	Black Pepper
cardamom	Coriander	Green
Ajwain	Cumin	Cardamom
Cayenne	Dill	Ajwain
Cinnamon	Fennel	Cayenne
Cloves	Ginger (fresh)	Cinnamon
Coriander	Mint	Cloves
Cumin	Parsley	Coriander
Dill	Saffron	Cumin
Fennel	Tarragon	Dill
Fenugreek	Turmeric	Fennel
Mint		Fenugreek
Garlic, Ginger		Garlic, Ginger
Mustard seeds		Mustard seeds
Nutmeg		Nutmeg
Oregano		Oregano
Paprika		Paprika
Parsley		Parsley
Poppy seeds		Poppy seeds
Rosemary		Rosemary
Saffron		Saffron
Star Anise		Star Anise
Tarragon		Tarragon
Thyme		Thyme
Turmeric		Turmeric

Spices and Pantry: Essentials and Well-stocked

Stock up on these spices and pantry "essentials" to get creative juices flowing. Then add "Well-stocked" items gradually if you cook regularly.

Spices Essentials:

Turmeric powder

Cumin powder

Coriander powder

Curry powder

Asafetida (Hing)

Garam masala powder

Himalayan pink salt

Whole cumin seeds

Whole black mustard seeds

Whole black pepper corns

Whole green cardamom pods

Fresh green cardamom powder (I grind my own every few weeks)

Whole Cloves

True cinnamon bark or Indian Dal-chinni (also called Cinnamomum zeylanicum or Cinnamomum verum). Bark looks broken, darker in color and is thinner compared to the cinnamon available in American markets, which is actually Cinnamon Cassia).

Cinnamon powder

Nutmeg powder

Rice vinegar

Apple-cider vinegar

Tamari

Soy Sauce

Spices well-stocked:
Dry meethi (fenugreek) leaves

Dry bay leaves (I dry my own)

Dry thyme leaves (I dry my own)

Dry sage leaves (I dry my own)

Black sesame seeds

White sesame seeds

Cayenne pepper powder

Tamarind paste

Pantry Essentials:
Ghee

Rice bran oil

Olive oil

Avocado oil

Toasted sesame oil

Olive oil

Basmati rice

Mixed 5 or 8 grains Asian rice

Quinoa

Split green mung lentils

Split yellow mung lentils

French green lentils (brown masoor)

Red lentils (chilka masoor)

Kidney beans

Garbanzo beans

Black beans

Potato starch

Pantry Well-stocked:

Whole green mung lentils

Yellow split pea lentils

Lima beans

Wild rice

Hemp seeds (need to be refrigerated)

Grounded flax (needs to be refrigerated)

Nutritional yeast

Traditional Indian Recipes

Simple Dal (lentils)

=Vata. =Pitta. =Kapha

1 cup yellow mung lentils

1½ inch ginger minced

3-4 cloves garlic

½ teaspoon coriander powder

pinch of hing (asafetida)

1 tablespoon whole cumin seeds

1 teaspoon black mustard seeds

10-12 fresh curry Leaves (optional) (available at Indian grocery stores)

Ghee

Salt to taste

Freshly grounded black pepper to taste

Chopped cilantro for garnish

Lemon or lime

- Pre-soak lentils in 4 cups water for 1 hour. Boil lentils until soft (about 15 minutes).

- While lentils are almost done, heat 1 tablespoon ghee in a frying pan on low heat.

- Add pinch of hing. Wait for few seconds.

- Add curry leaves if using and wait for about 30 seconds.

- Add whole cumin seeds and black mustard seeds. Cook until they start popping.

- Add minced garlic and ginger. Stir 30 seconds.

- Add coriander powder and mix thoroughly. Cook for about 2-3 minutes.

- Transfer to boiled lentils pot and mix all well. Add salt. Cook for 4-5 minutes. Close heat.

- If you are serving this as soup, you will need to add more water now to desired consistency. Bring it to a boil and then close heat.

- Ladle in a bowl or serve over rice. Garnish with a good amount of cilantro.

- Serve with lime/lemon.

Serve over Basmati rice or enjoy as quick soup.

Serves 2

Indian Mung Dal (Yellow Mung lentils)

-Vata. +Pitta. Slightly-Kapha

1 cup yellow mung lentils or split green mung lentils

1 red onion chopped

4-5 juicy Roma tomatoes chopped

3-4 cloves garlic minced

1½ inch ginger minced

¼ -½ minced Thai or Indian green chili to taste

1 teaspoon turmeric

½ teaspoon coriander powder

½ teaspoon cumin powder

pinch of hing (asafetida)

1 tablespoon whole cumin seeds

1 teaspoon black mustard seeds

10-12 fresh curry Leaves (optional) (available at Indian grocery stores)

Ghee

Salt to taste

Chopped cilantro for garnish

Lemon or lime

- Pre-soak lentils in 4 cups water for 1 hour. Boil lentils until soft (about 15 minutes) and set aside.

- Heat 3-4 tablespoons ghee in a deep pot.

- Add pinch of hing. Wait for few seconds.

- Add curry leaves if using and wait for about 30 seconds.

- Add whole cumin seeds and black mustard seeds. Cook until they start popping.

- Add minced garlic, ginger, chili. Stir 30 seconds.

- Add onions.

- When onions turn light brown (about 7-8 minutes), add coriander powder, cumin powder, turmeric, salt and mix thoroughly. Cook for about 1 minute.

- Add chopped tomatoes.

- Add boiled lentils and mix all well. Add more water if need a thinner consistency.

- Bring it to a boil. Then simmer on low heat for at least 30-35 minutes. Keep stirring and don't let lentils stick to the bottom of pan.

- Garnish with a good amount of cilantro.

- Serve with lime/lemon.

Serve over Basmati rice or serve as soup.

Serves 2

Indian Lal Masoor Dal (Red Lentils)

-Vata. +Pitta. -Kapha

1 cup red lentils

1 red onion chopped

3-4 juicy Roma tomatoes chopped

3-4 cloves garlic minced

1½ inch ginger minced

¼ -½ minced Thai or Indian green chili to taste

1 teaspoon turmeric

½ teaspoon coriander powder

½ teaspoon cumin powder

pinch of hing (asafetida)

1 tablespoon whole cumin seeds

Ghee

Salt to taste

Chopped cilantro for garnish

Lemon or lime

- Pre-soak lentils in 4 cups water for 30 minutes. Boil lentils until soft (about 15-20 minutes). Lentils will turn yellow on cooking. Set aside.

- Heat 3-4 tablespoons ghee in a deep pot.

- Add pinch of hing. Wait for few seconds.

- Add whole cumin seeds. Cook until they start popping.

- Add minced garlic, ginger and chili. Stir 30 seconds and add onions.

- When onions turn light brown (about 7-8 minutes), add coriander powder, cumin powder, turmeric, salt and mix thoroughly. Cook for about 1 minute.

- Add chopped tomatoes.

- Add boiled lentils and mix all well. Add more water if need a thinner consistency.

- Bring it to a boil. Then simmer on low heat for at least 30-35 minutes. Keep stirring and don't let lentils stick to the bottom of pan.

- Garnish with a good amount of cilantro.

- Serve with lime/lemon.

Serve over Basmati rice or serve as soup. Serves 2

Indian Kali Dal (Black Masoor or French lentils)

-Vata. +Pitta. -Kapha

1 cup French lentils

1 red onion chopped

3 juicy Roma tomatoes chopped

4-6 cloves garlic minced

1½ inch ginger minced

¼ -½ minced Thai or Indian green chili to taste

1 teaspoon turmeric

½ teaspoon coriander powder

½ teaspoon cumin powder

pinch of hing (asafetida)

1 tablespoon whole cumin seeds

1 teaspoon black mustard seeds

Salt to taste

Ghee

Chopped cilantro for garnish

Lemon or lime

- Pre-soak lentils in 5 cups water for about 2 hours. Boil lentils until soft (about 25-30 minutes) and set aside.

- Heat 3-4 tablespoons ghee in a deep pot.

- Add pinch of hing. Wait for few seconds.

- Add whole cumin seeds and black mustard seeds. Cook until they start popping.

- Add minced garlic, ginger and chili. Stir 30 seconds.

- Add onions. When onions turn light brown (about 7-8 minutes), add coriander powder, cumin powder, turmeric, salt, and mix thoroughly. Cook for about 1 minute.

- Add chopped tomatoes.

- Add boiled lentils and mix all well. Add more water if need a thinner consistency.

- Bring it to a boil. Then simmer on low heat for at least 30-40 minutes. Keep stirring and don't let lentils stick to the bottom of pan.

- Garnish with a good amount of cilantro.

- Serve with lime/lemon.

Serve over Basmati rice or serve as soup.

Serves 2

Kitchari

Kitchari is used for cleansing and detoxification, and used as mono-diet during Ayurvedic treatments (i.e. panchakarma), fasts and various cleanses throughout India.

=Vata. =Pitta. =Kapha

1 cup split yellow mung lentils

1 cup Basmati rice

6 cups water

1 red onion finely chopped

1½ inch ginger minced

¼ minced Thai or Indian green chili

1 teaspoon turmeric

½ teaspoon coriander powder

pinch of hing (Asafetida)

1 tablespoon whole cumin seeds

Salt to taste

Ghee

Chopped cilantro for garnish

- Pre-soak lentils and rice in 6 cups water for 1 hour.

- Heat 2-3 tablespoons ghee in a deep pot.

- Add pinch of hing. Cook for few seconds.

- Add whole cumin seeds, cook until they pop.

- Add minced ginger and chili. Stir 30 seconds.

- Add onions and sauté for about 7-8 minutes.

- When onions turn light brown, add coriander powder, turmeric, salt and stir thoroughly.

- Add lentils and rice with pre-measured water. Bring it to a boil. Then simmer on low heat until lentils are cooked and soft (about 30-40 minutes). Can add more water for a soupy consistency. Keep stirring every few minutes.

- Garnish with a good amount of cilantro.

Serves 2

Shazia's Kitchari

I LOVE Kitchari. I eat it all the times. For me, It is more than just a 'cleanse food'. I add some more spices and generous amount of vegetables. Each time it is different, depending on my mode and what vegetables are in season. Sometimes, I throw some spinach and sometimes a cup of boiled garbanzos.

I invite you to play with different veggies, beans and spices to discover your very own favorite.

-Vata. +Pitta. =Kapha

1 cup split yellow or green mung lentils

1 cup Basmati rice

6 cups water

1 red onion finely chopped

5 juicy Roma tomatoes chopped or roughly pureed

1½ inch ginger minced

4-5 cloves garlic minced

1 cup carrots sliced

½ cup green peas

½ cup yellow corn

3 cups (packed) spinach washed and cleaned

¼ minced Thai or Indian green chili

½ teaspoon turmeric

½ teaspoon coriander powder

1 teaspoon curry powder

pinch of hing (Asafetida)

1 tablespoon whole cumin seeds

Salt to taste

Ghee

½ teaspoon garam masala

2 tablespoon dry fenugreek (methi) leaves

Chopped cilantro for garnish

Lime

- Pre-soak lentils and rice in 6 cups water for 1 hour.

- Heat 2-3 tablespoons ghee in a deep pot.

- Add pinch of hing. Cook for few seconds.

- Add whole cumin seeds, cook until they pop.

- Add minced ginger, garlic and chili. Stir 30 seconds.

- Add onions and sauté for about 7-8 minutes.

- When onions turn light brown, add coriander powder, turmeric, curry powder, salt and stir thoroughly.

- Add lentils, rice, tomatoes and carrots with pre-measured water.

- Bring it to a boil. Close lid. Then simmer on low heat for about 30-35 minutes.

- Add peas, corn, spinach, garam masala and fenugreek leaves. Mix well. Stir and make sure it is sticking at the bottom of pan. Cook until lentils are fully cooked and soft (about 10 minutes). Keep stirring every few minutes.

- Garnish with a generous amount of cilantro. Serve with lime wedges.

Serves 4

Channa Dal Palak (Split pea lentils with spinach)

+Vata. =Pitta. =Kapha

½ cup yellow split pea lentils

1 medium red onion chopped

2 Roma tomatoes chopped

6 cups (packed) spinach, washed and coarsely chopped

5 cloves garlic minced

1½ inch ginger minced

¼ -½ minced Thai or Indian green chili to taste

½ teaspoon turmeric

½ teaspoon coriander powder

½ teaspoon cumin powder

2 pinches of hing (asafetida)

1 tablespoon whole cumin seeds

¼ teaspoon garam masala

Salt to taste

Ghee

Chopped cilantro for garnish

Lemon or lime

- Pre-soak lentils in 2 ½ cups water for 2 hours.

- Bring lentils to a boil. Then cook for 40-45 minutes on medium heat partially covered. Let all water evaporate. Lentils should be cooked but still hold its shape. Set aside.

- Heat 3-4 tablespoons ghee in a deep pot.

- Add 2 liberal pinches of hing. Cook for 1 minute.

- Add whole cumin seeds. Cook until they start popping.

- Add minced garlic, ginger and chili. Stir 30 seconds.

- Add onions. Sauté onions for about 6-7 minutes.

- When onions turn light brown, add coriander powder, cumin powder, turmeric, salt and stir thoroughly.

- Add tomatoes and boiled lentils and mix all well.

- Simmer on low heat for at least 30 minutes. Keep stirring and don't let lentils stick to the bottom of pan.

- Add garam masala. Mix well.

- Add spinach. Spinach will loose its volume and wilt very quickly. Cook for 5 minutes. Take off heat immediately. Do not over-cook spinach.

- Garnish with a good amount of cilantro.

- Serve with lime/lemon.

Traditionally served with roti (also called chapatti) or naan.

Serves 2

Palak (Spinach) Curry

=Vata. =Pitta. =Kapha

1 large bunch spinach, cleaned, stems removed and washed

1 red onion cut (big pieces OK)

4-5 juicy Roma tomatoes cut (big pieces OK)

1 green bell pepper cut in half and cleaned

6-7 cloves garlic minced

1½ inch ginger minced

¼ -½ minced Thai or Indian green chili to taste

1 teaspoon turmeric

1 teaspoon coriander powder

1 tablespoon whole cumin seeds

1 teaspoon black mustard seeds

½ teaspoon garam masala

pinch of hing (asafetida)

Salt to taste

Ghee

1 tablespoon thick Tamarind paste (optional). It is really sour.

1 cup paneer (Indian cottage cheese) cubes

- Boil 1 cup water. First place bell pepper and then spinach in water. Close the heat. Close the lid. Set aside.

- Heat 3-4 tablespoons ghee in a deep pot.

- Add pinch of hing.

- Add whole cumin seeds and black mustard seeds. Cook until they start popping.

- Add minced garlic, ginger and chili. Stir 30 seconds.

- Add onions. When onions turn light brown (about 7-8 minutes), add coriander powder, turmeric, salt, tamarind paste (optional) and stir thoroughly for 1 minute.

- Add tomatoes. Add boiled spinach and bell pepper with its water.

- Using an immersion blender, blend everything well.

- Add more water if need a thinner consistency.

- Bring it to a boil. Then simmer on low heat for at least 30 minutes. Keep stirring and don't let it stick to the bottom of pan.

- If using paneer or tofu cubes, add now.

- Add garam masala and cook for additional 10-15 minutes.

Traditionally served with roti (also called chapatti) or basmati rice.

Serves 4

Green Curry

=Vata. =Pitta. slightly+Kapha

1 large red onion cut (big pieces OK)

4-5 juicy Roma tomatoes cut (big pieces OK)

1 medium Yukon gold potatoes peeled and cut in medium cubes

2 cups fresh or frozen green peas

1 bunch spring onions (only green part)

1 large bunch cilantro (or 2 small) (stems OK)

½ bunch mint

4-5 cloves garlic minced

2 inch ginger minced

¼ -½ minced Thai or Indian green chili to taste

1 teaspoon turmeric

1 teaspoon coriander powder

1 tablespoon whole cumin seeds

1 teaspoon black mustard seeds

1 teaspoon curry powder

Salt to taste

Ghee

Chopped cilantro for garnish

Lemon or lime (optional)

- Heat 3-4 tablespoons ghee in a deep pot.

- Add whole cumin seeds and black mustard seeds. Cook until they start popping.

- Add minced garlic, ginger and chili. Stir 30 seconds.

- Add onions. Sauté for about 7-8 minutes.

- When onions turn light brown, add coriander powder, curry powder, turmeric, salt, and stir thoroughly for 1 minute.

- Add tomatoes, all greens and 3 cups of water.

- Using an immersion blender, blend everything well.

- Add potatoes.

- Bring it to a boil. Then simmer on low heat for at least 30 minutes.

- Keep stirring and don't let it stick to the bottom of pan.

- Add green peas and cook for additional 10 minutes.

- Garnish with good amount of cilantro.

- Serve with lemon or lime.

Traditionally served over basmati rice.

Serves 4

Aloo Matar (Potatoes and Green Peas) Light Curry

This recipe is altered from my mom's Pakistani mutton shorba to accommodate my vegetarian life style. Although it resembles traditional Indian Aloo Matar curry, inspiration of this dish actually comes from very Muslim and Pakistani staple "shorba". It is a staple in our house and reminds me of my roots and my mom.

For protein, sometimes I add boiled garbanzos beans while sometimes red kidney beans.

-Vata. +Pitta. slightly+Kapha.

1 red onion cut (big pieces OK)

5-6 juicy Roma tomatoes cut (big pieces OK)

2 medium Yukon gold potatoes peeled and cut in medium cubes

2 cups fresh or frozen green peas

4-5 cloves garlic minced

2 inch ginger minced

¼ -½ minced Thai or Indian green chili to taste

1 teaspoon turmeric

1 teaspoon coriander powder

1 teaspoon cumin powder

1 tablespoon whole cumin seeds

1 teaspoon black mustard seeds

½ teaspoon curry powder

Salt to taste

Ghee

Chopped cilantro for garnish

Lemon or lime (optional)

- Heat 3-4 tablespoons ghee in a deep pot.

- Add whole cumin seeds and black mustard seeds. Cook until they start popping.

- Add minced garlic, ginger and chili. Stir 30 seconds.

- Add onions. Sauté for about 7-8 minutes.

- When onions turn light brown, add coriander powder, cumin powder, curry powder, turmeric, salt, and stir thoroughly for 1 minute.

- Add tomatoes and 2 cups of water.

- Using an immersion blender, blend everything well. Add more water if need a thinner consistency.

- Add potatoes.

- Bring it to a boil. Then simmer on low heat for at least 30 minutes.

- Keep stirring and don't let it stick to the bottom of pan.

- Add green peas and cook for additional 10 minutes.

- Garnish with good amount of cilantro.

- Serve with lemon or lime.

Traditionally served over basmati rice.

Serves 4

Baingan (Eggplant) Bharta

=Vata. +Pitta. =Kapha.

2lbs Indian eggplants (small round ones, available in Indian and Asian food markets)

1 red onion cut (big pieces OK)

4 juicy Roma tomatoes cut (big pieces OK)

½ cup frozen green peas

4 sprigs green onions chopped thinly

6-7 cloves garlic chopped

1 inch ginger chopped

¼ -½ minced Thai or Indian green chili to taste

½ teaspoon turmeric

2 teaspoon coriander powder

1 teaspoon cumin powder

½ teaspoon madras curry powder

1 teaspoon black mustard seeds

Salt to taste

Ghee

2 teaspoons thick tamarind paste

- Wash and blot dry eggplants. Cut stems out. Pierce each eggplant few times with a fork. Broil for about 30 minutes. Turn at least 2 or more times.

- Heat 3-4 tablespoons ghee in a deep pot. Add garlic, ginger and chili. Stir 30 second.

- Add onion and sauté for about 7-8 minutes.

- Add black mustard seeds. Cook until they start popping.

- Add coriander powder, turmeric, cumin powder, madras curry powder, salt and stir thoroughly for 1 minute.

- Add tomatoes and broiled eggplants. Using an immersion blender, blend everything well.

- Add tamarind paste. Keep stirring until it is dissolved completely.

- Simmer on low heat for at least 30 minutes. Keep stirring.

- Add green peas and green onions and cook for additional 10 minutes until everything is smooth and velvety.

Traditionally served with roti (also called chapatti) or paratha.

Serves 4

Channa (Garbanzo) Masala

+Vata. +Pitta. Slightly+Kapha.

1 15-oz garbanzo can rinsed or 1 cup boiled garbanzo

1 red onion chopped

2 juicy Roma tomatoes chopped

1½ inch ginger minced

¼ -½ minced Thai or Indian green chili to taste

1 teaspoon cumin powder

1 tablespoon whole cumin seeds

1 tablespoon whole black mustard seeds

¼ teaspoon garam masala

pinch of hing (asafetida)

Salt to taste

Ghee

Chopped cilantro for garnish

1 teaspoon thick tamarind paste and ½ teaspoon brown sugar dissolved in it (optional). Tamarind is really sour and some people do not

like sour taste. Can use juice of ½ fresh lime instead.

- Heat 2-3 tablespoons ghee in a deep pot.

- Add pinch of hing.

- Add whole cumin seeds and black mustard seeds. Cook until they start popping.

- Add minced ginger and chili. Stir 30 seconds.

- Add onions. When onions turn translucent (about 5 minutes), add cumin powder and stir thoroughly for 1 minute.

- Add garbanzos, tomatoes, salt, ¼ cup water and tamarind paste (if using).

- Simmer on low heat for about 15 minutes. Keep stirring and don't let it stick to the bottom of pan.

- Add garam masala and cook for additional 5 minutes.

- Put in bowl. Garnish with generous amount of chopped cilantro. Add lime ONLY if you did not add tamarind paste.

Traditionally served with roti (also called chapatti) or poori (Indian fried bread). Can be enjoyed alone.

Serves 2

Chole (Garbanzo Appetizer)

Usually served as an appetizer, or enjoyed as a snack or served for entertaining guests, with chai. A staple in Pakistani and North-Indian homes! The names, "Channa Masala" and "Chole" are interchanged and confused easily.

+Vata. =Pitta. +Kapha

1 15-oz garbanzo can rinsed or 1 cup boiled garbanzo

1 red onion chopped

½ cup Yukon gold potatoes boiled and diced (optional)

¼ -½ minced Thai or Indian green chili to taste

1 teaspoon cumin powder

1 tablespoon whole cumin seeds

½ cup chopped cilantro

1 teaspoon thick tamarind paste

½ teaspoon brown sugar

¼ cup water

Salt to taste

Ghee or oil

- Heat 2-3 tablespoons ghee or oil in a deep pot.

- Add whole cumin seeds. Cook until they start popping.

- Add onions. Sauté until onions turn translucent, about 6 minutes.

- Reduce heat to low.

- Add cumin powder and stir thoroughly for 1 minute.

- In a small bowl, whisk tamarind paste, water and sugar until sugar is dissolved.

- Add green chili, salt, tamarind mixture to the pan and mix everything well.

- Add garbanzo and potatoes (if using). Mix gently.

- Simmer on low heat for about 10 minutes. Keep stirring.

- Put in bowl. Mix in chopped cilantro.

Serves 2

Black Bean Curry

+Vata. slightly+Pitta. +Kapha

1 cup black beans

1 medium red onion chopped

5-6 juicy Roma tomatoes chopped or pureed

8 cloves garlic minced

1 ½ inch ginger minced

¼ -½ minced Thai or Indian green chili to taste

1 teaspoon turmeric

1 teaspoon coriander powder

1 teaspoon curry powder

1½ tablespoon whole cumin seeds

1 tablespoon black mustard seeds

2 pinches of hing (Asafetida)

¼ teaspoon garam masala

Salt to taste

Ghee

Chopped cilantro for garnish

Lemon or lime

- Soak black beans over-night.

- Drain the water.

- Cooking on stove top: Add 4 cups water and cook in a covered pot until tender. May have to add more water. Do not drain any excess water.

- Cooking in a pressure cooker: Add 2 cups water and cook for 20 minutes. Do not drain water.

- Heat 3-4 tablespoons ghee in a deep pot.

- Add hing (Asafetida). Wait for it to get darker, about 1-2 minutes.

- Add whole cumin seeds and black mustard seeds. Cook until they start popping.

- Add minced garlic, ginger and chili. Stir 30 seconds and add onions.

- When onions turn light brown (about 7-8 minutes), add coriander powder, curry powder, turmeric, salt, and stir thoroughly for 1 minute.

- Add tomatoes, black beans with water and mix well.

- Bring it to a boil. Then simmer on low heat for 30 - 35 minutes.

- Keep stirring and don't let it stick to the bottom of pan.

- Add garam masala and cook for additional 5 minutes.

- Garnish with good amount of cilantro. Serve with lemon or lime.

Traditionally served over basmati rice.

Serves 2

Rajma (Red Kidney Beans Curry)

+Vata. slightly+Pitta. +Kapha

1 cup red kidney beans

1 medium red onion finely chopped

4-5 juicy Roma tomatoes roughly pureed

4 cloves garlic minced

2 inch ginger minced

¼ -½ minced Thai or Indian green chili to taste

1 teaspoon turmeric

1 teaspoon coriander powder

½ teaspoon cumin powder

½ teaspoon garam masala powder

1 tablespoon cumin seeds

2 pinches of hing (Asafetida)

3 bay leaves

Salt to taste

Ghee

Chopped cilantro for garnish

Lemon or lime

- Soak red kidney beans over-night.

- Drain the water.

- Cooking on stove top: Add 4 cups water and cook in a covered pot until tender. May have to add more water. Do not drain any excess water.

- Cooking in a pressure cooker: Add 2 cups water and cook for 20 minutes. Do not drain water.

- Heat 3-4 tablespoons ghee in a deep pot.

- Add hing (Asafetida). Wait few seconds for it to get darker in color.

- Add bay leaves and let it cook for 30 seconds.

- Add whole cumin seeds. Cook until they start popping.

- Add minced garlic, ginger and chili. Stir 30 seconds.

- Add onions. Sauté onions for about 7-8 minutes.

- When onions turn light brown, add coriander powder, cumin powder, turmeric, salt, and stir thoroughly for 1 minute.

- Add tomatoes, red kidney beans with water and mix well.

- Bring it to a boil. Then simmer on low heat for at least 40-45 minutes.

- Keep stirring and don't let it stick to the bottom of pan. Can add more water if needed. Beans should be soft. Curry should be thick and not runny.

- Add garam masala and cook for additional 5 minutes.

- Garnish with good amount of cilantro.

- Serve over white Basmati rice. Serve with lemon or lime.

Serves 2

Gobhi (Cauliflower) Sabzi

=Vata. =Pitta. =Kapha

1 small cauliflower head, flowers separated, stem removed (approx. 4 cups)

1 red onion chopped

2-3 Roma tomatoes chopped

1½ inch ginger minced

3 cloves garlic minced

¼ -½ minced Thai or Indian green chili to taste

1 potato cut in small pieces (optional)

1 teaspoon cumin powder

½ teaspoon coriander powder

1 teaspoon turmeric

1 tablespoon black mustard seeds

pinch of hing (Asafetida)

2 pinches of garam masala

Salt to taste

Ghee

Chopped cilantro for garnish

- Heat 3-4 tablespoons ghee in a wok or wide pan.

- Add Hing, wait for few seconds. Add black mustard seeds. Cook until they start popping.

- Add minced ginger, garlic and chili. Stir 30 seconds.

- Add onions. Sauté for about 6 minutes.

- When onions turn light brown, add cumin powder, coriander powder, turmeric, salt, and stir thoroughly for 1 minute.

- Add potatoes if using, cauliflower, tomatoes and mix everything well and simmer on low heat for about 15-20 minutes. Keep stirring and don't let it stick to the bottom of pan. (Can add more ghee now).

- Add garam masala. Simmer for another 10 minutes or until potatoes are soft.

- Garnish with chopped cilantro.

Traditionally served with roti (also called chapatti) or paratha. Can use Pita or flat bread instead. Serves 4.

Bhindi (okra) Aloo (potatoes) Sabzi

=Vata. =Pitta. slightly+Kapha

(avoid potatoes to make this recipe balancing for Kapha)

2 cups okra, washed, ends removed, cut in 1 inch pieces

1 medium red onion chopped

1 medium Yukon gold potato cut in cubes

3 Roma tomatoes chopped

1 ½ inch ginger minced

3 cloves garlic minced

¼ -½ minced Thai or Indian green chili to taste

½ teaspoon cumin powder

½ teaspoon coriander powder

1 teaspoon turmeric

1 tablespoon whole cumin seeds

Salt to taste

Ghee

Chopped cilantro for garnish

- Heat 4-5 tablespoons ghee in a wok or wide pan.

- Add whole cumin seeds. Cook until they start popping.

- Add minced ginger, garlic and chili. Stir 30 seconds.

- Add onions. When onions turn light brown (about 6 minutes), add cumin powder, coriander powder, turmeric, salt, and stir thoroughly for 1 minute.

- Add potatoes and cook for about 15 minutes.

- Add okra and tomatoes, mix everything well and simmer on low heat for about 20 minutes or until potatoes are soft. Keep stirring and don't let it stick to the bottom of pan. (can add more ghee if needed)

- Garnish with chopped cilantro.

Traditionally served with roti (also called chapatti) or paratha. Can eat with Pita or flat bread instead.

Serves 2

Aloo (potatoes) Baingan (eggplant) Sabzi

-Vata. ++Pitta. =Kapha

(avoid potatoes to make recipe balancing for Kapha)
10 small Indian eggplants (tiny ones, available in Indian and Asian food markets), tops removed and cut in 1" cubes

1½ medium or 1 large red onion chopped

2 medium Yukon gold potato cut in cubes

1½ inch ginger minced

6 cloves garlic minced

¼ -½ minced Thai or Indian green chili to taste

½ cup green peas

1½ teaspoon coriander powder

1 teaspoon turmeric

1 tablespoon whole cumin seeds

1 tablespoon dry fenugreek (meethi) leaves

Salt to taste

Ghee

Chopped cilantro for garnish

- Heat 4-5 tablespoons ghee in a wide pan.

- Add whole cumin seeds. Cook until they start popping.

- Add minced ginger, garlic and chili. Stir 30 seconds.

- Add onions. When onions turn light brown (about 6 minutes), add coriander powder, turmeric, salt, and stir thoroughly for 1 minute.

- Add potatoes and eggplants and mix everything well, so they are coated with spices.

- Cover and cook on low heat for about 30-35 minutes, turning them every few minutes.

- Add green peas and dry fenugreek leaves. Mix well and continue to cook on low heat for about 10 minutes or until potatoes are soft.

- Garnish with chopped cilantro.

Traditionally served with roti (also called chapatti) or paratha. Can eat with Pita or flat bread instead.

Serves 2

Mixed Vegetables Sabzi

=Vata. =Pitta. slightly+Kapha

½ cup carrots diced

½ cup green beans cut in 2"

½ cup green peas

½ cup potatoes

½ cup cauliflower or broccoli florets

½ cup shallots or sweet baby onions peeled

Any other vegetables of your choice

1 med. red onion chopped

1½ inch ginger minced

4 cloves garlic minced

¼ -½ minced Thai or Indian green chili to taste

1 teaspoon coriander powder

1 teaspoon cumin powder

1 teaspoon turmeric

1 tablespoon whole cumin seeds

Ghee

Salt to taste

1 stem green onion sliced for garnish

½ cup chopped cilantro for garnish

- Heat 4-5 tablespoons ghee in a wok or wide pan.

- Add whole cumin seeds. Cook until they start popping.

- Add minced ginger, garlic and chili. Stir 30 seconds.

- Add onions. When onions become translucent (6 minutes. Do not over-cook onions), add cumin powder, coriander powder, turmeric, salt, and stir thoroughly for 1 minute.

- Add potatoes and carrots. Mix everything well and cook on **low heat** for about 20 minutes. Keep stirring and turning every few minutes and don't let it stick to the bottom of pan. Add more ghee if spices and veggies start to stick at the bottom of pan.

- Add green beans. Mix slowly, without breaking vegetables. Cook for about 10 minutes.

- Add all other vegetables. Mix slowly. Cook for another 5-10 minutes on low heat turning constantly, until all veggies are soft.

- Garnish with green onions and cilantro.

Traditionally, served with roti, chapatti or parantha.

Serves 4

Zeera (cumin seeds) Aloo (potatoes) Sabzi

-Vata. -Pitta. +Kapha

3 Yukon gold potatoes cut in 1" cubes

1 med. red onion chopped

1½ inch ginger minced

1 teaspoon coriander powder

½ teaspoon turmeric powder

1 tablespoon whole cumin seeds

Ghee

Salt to taste

Freshly grated black pepper to taste

1 stem green onion sliced for garnish

½ cup chopped cilantro for garnish

- Heat 4-5 tablespoons ghee in a wok or wide pan.

- Add whole cumin seeds. Cook until they start popping.

- Add minced ginger. Stir 30 seconds.

- Add onions. When onions become translucent (5-6 minutes. Do not over-cook onions), add cumin powder, coriander powder, salt, and stir thoroughly for 1 minute.

- Add potatoes. Mix everything well and cook on **low heat** for about 30-40 minutes until potatoes are soft. Add more ghee if spices and veggies start to stick at the bottom of pan. Keep stirring and turning every few minutes and don't let it stick to the bottom of pan.

- Garnish with green onions and chopped cilantro.

Traditionally served with roti (also called chapatti) or paratha.

Serves 2

Methi (Fenugreek leaves) Aloo (potatoes) Sabzi

Fenugreek leaves have a bitter taste which reduces Kapha. They are available at Indian and Middle Eastern grocery stores and are seasonal. Make sure you use fenugreek leaves and not seeds.

Slightly+Vata. -Pitta. =Kapha

(avoid potatoes to decrease Kapha)

2 cups packed fenugreek leaves, ends removed, washed

1 medium red onion chopped

1 large Yukon gold potato cut in ½" cubes

3 Roma tomatoes chopped

½ cup frozen green peas

1½ inch ginger minced

3 cloves garlic minced

¼ -½ minced Thai or Indian green chili to taste

Pinch of hing (Asafetida)

1 teaspoon coriander powder

1 teaspoon curry powder

½ teaspoon turmeric

1 tablespoon black mustard seeds

Salt to taste

Ghee

Chopped cilantro for garnish

- Heat 4-5 tablespoons ghee in a wok or wide pan.

- Add hing (Asafetida). Wait few seconds for it to get darker in color.

- Add whole black mustard seeds. Cook until they start popping.

- Quickly, add minced ginger, garlic and chili. Stir 30 seconds.

- Add onions. When onions turn light brown (about 6 minutes), add curry powder, coriander powder, turmeric, salt, and stir thoroughly for 1 minute.

- Add potatoes and cook on low heat until potatoes are 90% cooked (about 20-25 minutes) all this while stirring constantly. (can add more ghee if needed)

- Add fenugreek leaves and mix in well. Cook until leaves lose their volume (about 5 minutes).

- Add tomatoes and green peas, mix everything very well and simmer on low heat for about 8-10 minutes or until potatoes are soft. Keep stirring and don't let it stick to the bottom of pan.

- Garnish with chopped cilantro.

Traditionally served with roti ((also called chapatti) or paratha. Can eat with Pita or flat bread instead.

Serves 2

Lauki (Indian bottle gourd) Channa Dal Sabzi

=Vata. =Pitta. =Kapha

3 cups lauki peeled and cut in 1" cubes

1 cup yellow split pea lentils

1 large red onion chopped

4 juicy red tomatoes chopped

1 ½ inch ginger minced

5-6 cloves garlic minced

¼ -½ minced Thai or Indian green chili to taste

1 teaspoon coriander powder

1 teaspoon cumin powder

1 teaspoon turmeric

1 tablespoon whole cumin seeds

2 pinches of hing (asafetida)

¼ teaspoon garam masala

4-5 bay leaves

Ghee

Salt to taste

Juice of 1 large lemon or lime

Chopped cilantro for garnish

2 sprigs green onions thinly sliced (green part only)

- Pre-soak lentils in 2 ½ cups water for 2 hours.

- Bring lentils to a boil. Then cook for 40-45 minutes on medium heat partially covered. Let all water evaporate. Lentils should be cooked but still hold its shape. Set aside.

- Heat 3-4 tablespoons ghee in a wok or wide pan.

- Add bay leaves and whole cumin seeds. Cook until cumin seeds start popping.

- Add minced ginger, garlic and chili. Stir 30 seconds.

- Add onions. When onions turn light brown (about 6 minutes), add coriander powder, cumin powder, turmeric, salt, and stir thoroughly for 1 minute.

- Add lauki and mix everything well, so lauki pieces are coated with spices.

- Add lentils and tomatoes. Mix. Cover and cook on medium-low heat for about 10 minutes, turning it every few minutes.

- Reduce heat to low and continue to cook for another 10 minutes turning it every few minutes.

- Lauki will release its water; you want to leave some liquid in the dish. Do not dry out the dish.

- Add garam masala and lime. Mix well. Cook for another 6-10 minutes. When lauki is mushy, it is done.

- Garnish with chopped cilantro and green onions. Serve with more lemon or lime wedges.

Traditionally served with roti (also called chapatti) or paratha.

Serves 6

Karela (Indian bitter gourd or bitter melon) Sabzi

Karela's health benefits are numerous. Karela's bitter taste reduces Kapha. Ayurvedically, Karela is celebrated to cleanse blood, digestive organs, respiratory organs, and reduce weight.

Karela:
- resolve heat and damp from blood.
- detoxifies heart, liver, spleen, kidneys.
- detoxifies bile.
- decreases high blood sugar so helps with diabetes-II.
- heals ulcers and skin diseases.

Karela is available at Indian and Asian grocery stores and is seasonal.

slightly+Vata. --Pitta. −Kapha

1 lb Karela (Indian bitter gourd)

1 medium yellow onion chopped

3 Roma tomatoes chopped

½ cup yellow corn

1½ inch ginger minced

6 cloves garlic minced

¼ -½ minced Thai or Indian green chili to taste

1 teaspoon coriander powder

½ teaspoon turmeric

½ teaspoon curry powder

1 teaspoon whole cumin seeds

Salt to taste

Ghee

Chopped cilantro for garnish

- Peel Karela until all dark green hard skin is removed and smooth light-green color appears. (Be patient)

- Wash karela. Mix 3 Tablespoon salt in a 3 cups of water in a large bowl. Soak karela in salt water for 30 minutes.

- Heat 4-5 tablespoons ghee in a wok or wide pan.

- Add whole cumin seeds. Cook until they start popping.

- Quickly, add minced ginger, garlic and chili. Stir 30 seconds.

- Add onions.

- While onions are cooking, discard water from bowl and pat dry karela completely. Then cut in slices. Keep aside.

- When onions turn light brown (about 6 minutes), add curry powder, coriander powder, turmeric, salt, and stir thoroughly for 1 minute.

- Turn heat to low. Add karela and cook on low heat turning them every few minutes. Don't let spices and onions stick at the bottom of pan. Can add more ghee if needed. Cook for 15 minutes.

- Add tomatoes and corn. Mix and simmer on low heat until all tomatoes liquid is evaporated and karela is soft (about 20-30 minutes).

- Try one of the karela pieces to see if it is cooked. It will NOT get very soft, but you should be able to bite into it without effort. If it is, karela is done. Otherwise continue to cook on low heat until done.

- Take off heat, garnish with chopped cilantro.

Traditionally served with roti (also called chapatti) or paratha. Can eat with Pita or flat bread instead.

Serves 2

Pav Bhaji (Bombay-style Mashed Potatoes)

Some of world's best and cheapest food is available in Bombay. This is a famous street food for the poor of Bombay. It is traditionally served with buns. It also makes good stuffing for sandwiches that will last a long time.

=Vata. =Pitta. +Kapha

1 med red onion chopped

2-3 juicy Roma tomatoes chopped

2 medium Yukon gold potatoes boiled, skinned and mashed (or potatoes of your choice)

1 cup fresh or frozen green peas

4 cloves garlic minced

1 inch ginger minced

¼ -½ minced Thai or Indian green chili to taste

1 teaspoon turmeric

½ teaspoon coriander powder

1 tablespoon whole cumin seeds

pinch of hing (Asafetida)

Salt to taste

Ghee

1-2 teaspoon tamarind paste OR lime (as per your taste)

Garnish:

½ cup chopped cilantro for generous garnish

2 sprigs green onions (green part only) thinly sliced for garnish

- Heat 3-4 tablespoons ghee in a deep pot.

- Add hing and wait for few seconds.

- Add whole cumin seeds. Cook until they start popping.

- Add minced garlic, ginger and chili. Stir 30 seconds.

- Add onions. When onions turn light brown (about 5-6 minutes), add coriander powder, turmeric, salt, and stir thoroughly for 1 minute.

- Add mashed potatoes and tomatoes and mix everything very well.

- Simmer on low heat for about 30 minutes stirring constantly. Do not let it stick to the bottom of pan.

- Add more ghee if potatoes are sticking to the bottom of pan.

- If using tamarind paste, add now and mix it very well.

- Add green peas and cook for additional 10 minutes.

- Remove from heat.

- If using lime, add now as per taste and mix well.

- Garnish with generous amount of cilantro and green onions. This dish is tangy to taste.

Traditionally served with buns. Can enjoy with roti (also called chapatti), paratha, Pita, flat bread or regular bread.

Serves 2

Paneer (Indian cheese) Bhurji

=Vata. =Pitta. ++Kapha

2 cups paneer (Indian cheese) can be bought at Indian store)

1 red onion chopped

3 Roma tomatoes chopped

2 inch ginger minced

6 cloves garlic minced

¼ -½ minced Thai or Indian green chili to taste

1 bunch green onions chopped – whites and greens separated

1 cup frozen green peas

1 teaspoon cumin powder

1 teaspoon coriander powder

1 teaspoon turmeric

1 tablespoon cumin seeds

Salt to taste

Ghee

½ cup chopped cilantro for garnish

- Heat 4-5 tablespoons ghee in a wide pan.
- Add cumin seeds. Cook until they start popping.
- Add minced ginger, garlic and chili. Stir 30 seconds.
- Add onions and sauté for 6-7 minutes.
- While onions are cooking, grate paneer or crumble it with bare hands into tiny pieces (since it is a soft cheese, it is very easy to loosen).
- When onions turn light brown, add cumin powder, coriander powder, turmeric, salt, and stir thoroughly for 1 minute.
- Add paneer and tomatoes, mix everything very well. Simmer on low heat for about 15 minutes. Keep stirring and don't let it stick to the bottom of pan. (can add more ghee now).
- Add green peas. Cook for another 5-10 minutes.
- Garnish with chopped cilantro.

Traditionally served with roti (also called chapatti) or paratha. Can eat with Pita or flat bread.

Serves 2

Matar Zeera Brown Pulaoo (Rice)

=Vata. =Pitta. +Kapha

1 cup white Basmati rice

2 cups water

½ red onion chopped

1 cup green peas

1 green cardamom seeded

1 tablespoon cumin seeds

Ghee

Salt to taste

- Heat 1 tablespoon ghee in a pot.
- Add whole cumin seeds. Cook until they start popping.
- Add green cardamom seeds.
- Add onions and sauté until light brown, about 7-8 minutes.

- Add green peas, water, rice, salt and stir well.

- Close the lid. Bring it to a boil. Then cook on low heat for 14-15 minutes until rice is done. Do NOT open the lid during this time. Can open after 14-15 minutes to make sure rice is cooked.

Traditionally served with curry dishes, lentils or gravy dishes. Can be enjoyed with one of the raitas.

Serves 2

Garam Masala Pulaoo

-Vata. Slightly+Pitta. Slightly+Kapha

1 cup white Basmati rice

2 cups water

5-6 green cardamom (seeds removed, pods discarded)

3-4 cloves

2 sticks Indian cinnamon

1 tablespoon cumin seeds

Ghee

Salt to taste

- Heat 2 teaspoons ghee in a pot.

- Add whole cumin seeds. Cook until they start popping.

- Add all spices and cook until fragrant.

- Add water, rice, salt and stir well.

- Close the lid. Bring it to a boil. Then cook on low heat until rice is done (about 14-15 minutes). Do NOT open the lid during this time. Can open after 14-15 minutes to make sure rice is cooked. Rice should be separate and not sticking together.

Traditionally served with curry dishes, lentils or gravy dishes. Can be enjoyed with one of the raitas.

Serves 2

Punjabi Channa (Garbanzo) Pulaoo (Rice)

+Vata. Slightly+Pitta. +Kapha

1 cup white Basmati rice

2 cups water

½ yellow onion chopped length-wise

1 cup boiled garbanzo beans

1 small stick Indian cinnamon

1 tablespoon cumin seeds

pinch of garam masala

Ghee

Salt to taste

- Heat 1 tablespoon ghee in a pot.

- Add cinnamon stick and whole cumin seeds. Cook until cumin seeds start popping.

- Add onions and sauté until light brown, about 7-8 minutes.

- Add garbanzo beans, water, rice, salt, garam masala and stir well.

- Close the lid. Bring it to a boil. Then cook on low heat for 14-15 minutes until rice is done. Do NOT open the lid during this time. Can open after 14-15 minutes to make sure rice is cooked.

Traditionally served with curry dishes, lentils or gravy dishes. Can be enjoyed with one of the raitas.

Serves 2

Vegetable Pulaoo (Rice)

-Vata. =Pitta. +Kapha

1 cup white Basmati rice

2 cups water

½ red onion cut length-wise

½ cup green peas

½ cup green beans cut in 2"

½ cup potatoes peeled and cubed

½ cup carrots diced

½ cup cauliflower

Any other vegetables of your choice

1 cup garbanzo beans

2-3 green cardamoms seeded

2 Indian cinnamon sticks

3-4 whole cloves

1 tablespoon cumin seeds

Pinch of garam masala

Ghee

Salt to taste

- Heat 2 teaspoons ghee in a pot.

- Add whole cumin seeds. Cook until they start popping.

- Add green cardamom seeds, cinnamon stick, and cloves. Let it heat for 1-2 minutes until fragrant.

- Add onions and sauté until brown, about 7-8 minutes

- Add all vegetables, garbanzo beans, water, rice, salt, garam masala powder and stir well.

- Close the lid. Bring it to a boil. Then cook on low heat for about 15-20 minutes, until rice is cooked. Do NOT open the lid during this time. Can open after 15 minutes to check if rice is done or need more time. Do not over-cook rice. Rice should be long, soft and non-sticky.

Can be served with plain yogurt or one of the raitas.

Serves 2

Mughlai Pulaoo (Rice)

-Vata. Slightly+Pitta. +Kapha

1 cup white Basmati rice

2 cups water

6-8 green cardamom (seeds removed, pods discarded)

3-4 cloves

2 sticks Indian cinnamon

1 teaspoon cumin seeds

½ cup unsalted sliced nuts (almonds, cashews, pistachios, pine nuts)

¼ cup dry berries (golden raisins, cranberries, goji berries)

Few strands of saffron

Ghee

Salt to taste

- Heat 2 teaspoons ghee in a pot.
- Add whole cumin seeds. Cook until they start popping.

- Add all spices, nuts and berries and cook until fragrant.

- Add water, rice, salt and stir well.

- Close the lid. Bring it to a boil. Then cook on low heat for about 14-15 minutes, until rice is cooked. Do NOT open the lid during this time. Can open after 14 or 15 minutes to make sure rice is done. Rice should be separate and not sticking together.

Traditionally served with curry dishes or gravy dishes. Serve with plain yogurt or one of the raitas.

Serves 2

Mughlai Vegetable and Paneer Biryani (Rice)

Mughlai Biryani is a royal dish, cooked elaborately to please a king's palate. It is a beloved celebratory dish proudly served at special occasions and for distinguished guests. This dish is famous among all south-Asians, Iranians and Arabs. There are as many versions of biryani as many countries in south Asia and each region have developed its own version of biryani. Different styles of biryani may include mutton, lamb, chicken, beef, fish, paneer (Indian cheese), yogurt, nuts, raisins, boiled eggs, etc. Some regions use revered and expensive saffron, while other may use ordinary food colors; some may use cilantro as a garnish while others love fried crispy onions, etc.

Biryani is traditionally made with meat. I have customized my own unique vegetarian version that I adapted from my mother's traditional mutton biryani – which is by far the most delicious biryani I have ever tasted.

Biryani is a very traditional meal and takes patience to create a dish with all the complex layering of flavors. Think of it as circumstances related to the traditional Thanksgiving Turkey preparation. I cook it for special occasions only, while my mother proudly servers it every weekend. Set aside 2.5 - 3 hours. It requires patience.

-Vata. +Pitta. +Kapha

2 cups white Basmati rice

4½ cups water

1 large red onion chopped

7-8 very juicy Roma tomatoes chopped

1 cup frozen green peas

1 cup green beans cut in 2″

1 cup potatoes peeled and cubed

1 cup carrots sliced

1 cup cauliflower florets

1 cup green bell pepper cut in 1″ cubes

1 cup cubed paneer (Indian cheese, can be bought at Indian grocery store). Avoid if vegan.

1 cup boiled red kidney beans

1 cup full-cream plain yogurt

1 med red onion chopped length-wise

8 cloves garlic minced

2 inch ginger minced

1 Thai or Indian green chili minced

8 green cardamoms seeded

4-5 Indian cinnamon sticks

8 whole cloves

5-6 bay leaves

2 teaspoon cumin seeds

1 teaspoon cumin powder

1 teaspoon coriander powder

1 teaspoon turmeric

½ teaspoon garam masala powder

¼ teaspoon nutmeg powder

Few strands of saffron (optional)

Ghee

Salt to taste

- Heat 4-5 tablespoon ghee in a pot.
- Add whole cumin seeds. Cook until they start popping.
- Add green cardamom seeds, cinnamon stick, cloves and bay leaves. Let it heat for 2-3 minutes until fragrant.

- Add ginger, garlic, green chili and sauté for about 1 minute.

- Add onions and sauté until they turn brown, about 7-8 minutes.

- Add cumin powder, coriander powder, turmeric, nutmeg powder, garam masala powder, salt, and stir thoroughly for 1-2 minutes.

- Add potatoes and cook for 5-6 minutes. Keep stirring constantly so they don't stick at bottom.

- Add tomatoes and all vegetables except green peas and mix well. Cook on medium-low heat uncovered until vegetables are half cooked (about 30-35 minutes), turning them occasionally.

- While vegetables are cooking, in a separate frying pan, heat 2 tablespoon ghee and sauté onions that are cut length-wise until onions turn dark brown and crisp.

- There should be no ghee left in onions. If there is any extra ghee, drain it in a small bowl. Let onions cool down for few minutes.

- In a mixing bowl whisk yogurt. Add crisped onions to the bowl and mix thoroughly.

- Then add green peas and paneer to the pot and mix slowly. Cook for another 5-10 minutes.

- Close heat. Now add red kidney beans and yogurt-onions mix in the vegetables pan and mix thoroughly.

- Wash rice. Transfer it to a separate pan, add 4½ cups water, few drops of ghee and boil it uncovered until rice is Al-dente. Rice should be only 90% cooked. Strain rice and let extra water drain out.

- On very low heat, melt 1-2 teaspoons ghee to grease a large deep pot. Set in half of the rice as first layer. Then layer all of the vegetables-paneer-beans gravy on top of rice as second layer. Then layer rest of the rice on top as third layer. Drizzle few teaspoons of melted ghee at top.

- Mix saffron in 4 tablespoons of water and drizzle very slowly (and patiently) at top of rice evenly (this step is optional).

- Cover a tight-fitted lid thoroughly with aluminum foil so moisture can be sealed inside. Seal the pot and cook for 20 minutes on simmer. (It is very important to use **lowest heat setting or simmer**, otherwise everything will burn). DO NOT open the lid to check.

- After 20 minutes, open lid and check rice. Rice should cooked, still long and separate from each other and NOT mushy. If rice is undercooked, cover tightly again and cook for another 5 minutes.

- Place Biryani in wide dinner plates. Serve with one of the yogurt raitas.

Serves 4

South-Indian Tomato Rice

Traditionally, this dish is cooked with lots of dried red chilies. Well, we are not doing that. With my sincere apologies to South-Indians, so much chili (especially powered red chili) is not good for your stomach lining.

-Vata. +Pitta. +Kapha.

1½ cups white Basmati rice

3½ cups water

1 med red onion chopped

5 (about 3 cups) juicy Roma tomatoes pureed

1 cup carrots cut in slices

1 cup frozen green peas

1 cup green beans cut in 2"

1 cup paneer (Indian cheese) cubes (optional)

6 cloves garlic chopped

1 inch ginger chopped

¼ -½ minced Thai or Indian green chili to taste

Few fresh Indian Curry Leaves (available at Indian grocery store. If Indian store is far, don't worry looking for it. It will not make or break this dish. It is more for fragrance)

1 teaspoon Madras curry powder

½ teaspoon coriander powder

¼ teaspoon garam masala

1 teaspoon black mustard seeds

Juice of ½ lime

Salt to taste

Ghee

Chopped cilantro for garnish

- Heat 3-4 tablespoons ghee in a deep pot.

- Add black mustard seeds and curry leaves (if using). Cook until mustard seeds start popping.

- Add garlic, ginger and chili. Stir for 30 seconds.

- Add onions. When onions turn light brown (7-8 minutes), add coriander powder, madras curry powder, garam masala, salt, and stir thoroughly for 1 minute.

- Add tomatoes, water, rice, all vegetables, lime, salt and panner (if using).

- Bring it to a boil. Then cook on low heat for 15 minutes.

- After 15 minutes, stir thoroughly. Cook for another 5 minutes.

- Rice should be done and soft.

- If rice is not done, continue cooking for few more minutes on low heat.

- Serve immediately. Garnish with cilantro.

Serves 4

Cooling Green Raita (Yogurt)

(Avoid this recipe in winter)

slightly+Vata. --Pitta. ++Kapha

1 cup plain yogurt

½ cucumber peeled and grated

½ cup cilantro finely chopped

¼ cup fresh mint finely chopped

2 sprigs green onions chopped in thin slices

1 teaspoon cumin seeds

Himalayan pink salt to taste

Freshly grounded black pepper to taste

- In a pan, dry roast cumin seeds for about 5 minutes stirring few times. Close heat. Let it cool for few minutes.

- Whisk the yogurt alone in a bowl.

- Add all ingredients and mix well.

- Adjust salt and pepper.

Serves 2

Punjabi / Pakistani Raita (Yogurt)

slightly+Vata. -Pitta. +Kapha

1 cup plain yogurt

½ cucumber peeled and chopped

1 medium firm red tomato chopped

¼ red onion chopped

½ cup cilantro chopped

1 teaspoon cumin seeds

Himalayan pink salt to taste

Freshly grounded black pepper to taste

- In a pan, dry roast cumin seeds for about 5 minutes stirring few times. Close heat. Let it cool for few minutes.

- Whisk the yogurt alone in a bowl.

- Add all ingredients and mix well.

- Adjust salt and pepper.

Serves 2

Aloo (potatoes) Raita (Yogurt)

slightly+Vata. -Pitta. ++Kapha

1 cup plain yogurt

1 medium gold potato

¼ cup cilantro chopped

Himalayan pink salt to taste

½ teaspoon freshly grounded black pepper

¼ teaspoon garam masala

- Boil the potato in water. Potato should be cooked but not mushy. Take it out of water. Let it cool. Once cooled, peel and grate.

- Whisk the yogurt alone in a bowl.

- Add all ingredients and mix well.

- Adjust salt and pepper.

Serves 2

Anar (pomegranate) Raita (Yogurt)

+Vata. -Pitta. +Kapha

1 cup plain yogurt

½ cup pomegranate seeds

Himalayan pink salt to taste

Freshly grounded black pepper to taste

- Whisk the yogurt alone in a bowl.

- Add salt and pepper and taste it. Adjust.

- Add pomegranate seeds.

Serves 2

Channna (Garbanzo) Chat (raw salad)

This is most loved street food sold all over North India and served in every Indian and Pakistani home for fun, entertainment, as quick snack, sometimes eaten with chai.

When my life gets hectic and I need to fix quick lunch (and when I am avoiding bread), I fix this in few minutes. I always keep few garbanzo cans in my pantry. This never got boring no matter how often we eat this.

+Vata. Slightly+Pitta. +Kapha

1 15-oz garbanzo can rinsed or 1 cup boiled garbanzo

¼ red onion chopped or 2 springs of green onions chopped

2 juicy Roma tomatoes chopped

1 tablespoon whole cumin seeds

Few dashes of garam masala (optional)

Himalayan pink salt to taste

Freshly grounded black pepper to taste

½ cup cilantro chopped

Juice of ½ - 1 Lemon or Lime

- In a pan, dry roast cumin seeds for about 5 minutes flipping few times. Let it cool for few minutes.

- In a large bowl, add all ingredients and mix very well.

- Adjust lemon or lime. Chat should be tangy.

Serves 2

Try other variations:

- Add ¼ cup chopped Italian parsley.

- Add red kidney beans, chopped red peppers, or sweet corn.

Green Chutney

+Vata . +Pitta. -Kapha

2 bunches cilantro washed and cleaned

1 small bunch fresh mint washed and cleaned

1 juicy red Roma tomato

½ - 1 fresh Thai or Indian green chili to taste

Juice of ½ small lime

Himalayan pink salt to taste

Freshly grounded black pepper to taste

- In a blender, first place tomato, then all other ingredients.
- Blend all ingredients until it turns into a smooth paste. (Can add few drops of water if your blender needs more liquid).
- Taste and adjust salt, pepper and lime if needed.

Red Hot Chutney

slightly+Vata . ++Pitta. -Kapha

1 medium red onion

2-3 cloves garlic peeled

1" ginger peeled

½ - 1 fresh Thai or Indian green chili to taste

½ bunch cilantro washed and cleaned

½ small bunch fresh mint washed and cleaned

1 teaspoon unsweetened tamarind paste

cayenne pepper to taste

Salt to taste

- In a blender, place everything except cilantro and mint and blend well.
- Add greens. Blend until it turns into a smooth paste. (Can add few drops of water if your blender needs more liquid).
- Taste and adjust salt and pepper if needed.

Masala Chai

This masala (spicy) chai is good for cold wintery and rainy days. It is warming in nature, nurturing and soothing. No matter how often people come to my cooking workshops, chai never gets boring. Sometimes, I have big pots of chai boiling even before they arrive (I know it will never go wasted).

I make it from scratch few times a day. Yes, I am addicted to chai.

-Vata. +Pitta. −Kapha

1½ cup water

½" fresh ginger grated or chopped

2 green cardamom seeded or 1/8 teaspoon green cardamom powder (I grind mine fresh every about every 2 weeks)

1-2 clove

1 small stick Indian cinnamon (optional)

1 teaspoon loose Indian black tea (Orange Pekoe, Assam or Ceylon)

Few tablespoons Half/Half or ¼ cup almond milk (for vegan alternative)

Sweetener of your choice (optional)

- Boil ginger in water for at least 5 minutes.

- Add loose tea and all spices. Close the heat, lid and let it steep for 6-8 minutes.

- Strain in the cup.

- Add milk of your choice.

- Add your choice of sweetener if you like sweet taste.

Serves 1

Kapha Pacifying Chai

1½ cup water

½" fresh ginger grated or chopped

1-2 clove or 1/8 teaspoon clove powder

1 small stick Indian cinnamon

6-8 whole black pepper corns

1 teaspoon loose Indian black tea (Orange Pekoe, Assam or Ceylon)

Few tablespoons Half/Half or ¼ cup almond milk (for vegan alternative)

Honey to taste (optional)

- Boil ginger in water for at least 5 minutes.
- Add loose tea and all spices. Close the heat, lid and let it steep for 6-8 minutes.
- Strain in the cup.
- Add milk of your choice.
- Add honey if you like sweet taste.

    Serves 1

Pitta Pacifying Chai

1½ cup water

2 green cardamom seeded or 1/8 teaspoon green cardamom powder (I grind mine fresh every about every 2 weeks)

1 tablespoon fennel seeds

1 tablespoon rose petals

1 teaspoon dry mint leaves

1 teaspoon loose Indian black tea (Orange Pekoe, Assam or Ceylon)

Few tablespoons Half/Half or ¼ cup almond milk

Sweetener of your choice (optional)

- Add loose tea and fennel to boiling water. Boil for 5-6 minutes on low heat.

- Add rose petals, dry mint and green cardamom. Close the heat, lid and let it steep for 5 minutes.

- Strain in the cup.

- Add milk of your choice.

- Add your choice of sweetener if you like sweet taste.

Serves 1

Vata Pacifying Chai

1½ cup water

½" fresh ginger grated or chopped

2 green cardamom seeded or 1/8 teaspoon green cardamom powder (I grind mine fresh every about every 2 weeks)

1-2 clove or 1/8 teaspoon clove powder

1 small stick Indian Cinnamon (optional)

¼ teaspoon Ajwain (carom) seeds

¼ teaspoon nutmeg powder

1 teaspoon loose Indian black tea (Orange Pekoe, Assam or Ceylon).

Few tablespoons Half/Half or ¼ cup almond milk (for vegan alternative)

Sweetener of your choice (optional).

- Boil ginger in water for at least 5 minutes.

- Add loose tea and all spices. Close the heat, lid and let it steep for 6-8 minutes.

- Strain in the cup.

- Add milk of your choice.

- Add your choice of sweetener if you like sweet taste.

Serves 1

Ginger Digestive Tea

1½ cup water

1" fresh ginger grated or chopped

2-3 green cardamom seeded 1/8 teaspoon green cardamom powder (I grind mine fresh every about every 2 weeks)

1 teaspoon fennel seeds

- Boil ginger in water covered for at least 10 minutes.

- Add all spices. Close the heat, lid and let it steep for 5-6 minutes.

- Strain in the cup.

Serves 1

Kasmhiri Kahwa

-Vata. slightly+Pitta. −Kapha

1½ cup water

2 green cardamom seeded or 1/8 teaspoon freshly-grounded green cardamom powder

1 clove

1 small stick Indian cinnamon (optional)

Few strands of saffron

1 teaspoon loose green tea (green Darjeeling)

Sweetener of your choice (optional)

- Boil all spices in water except saffron for at least 5 minutes.

- Add loose tea in water.

- Close the heat, lid and let it steep for 5-6 minutes.

- Dissolve saffron in few tablespoons of water separately.

- Strain the tea in cup and saffron.

- Add your choice of sweetener if you like sweet taste.
  Serves 1

Lassi (Indian Yogurt drink)

This can be served cold or room temperature.

slightly+Vata. -Pitta. ++Kapha

½ cup plain yogurt

1½ cup room-temp water

Pinch of cumin powder

Himalayan pink salt to taste

Freshly grounded black pepper to taste

- Whisk the yogurt very well with water in a bowl until frothy.

- Add salt and pepper. Mix and pour in a glass.

- Add pinch of cumin powder at top.

Serves 1

Mango Lassi (Indian Yogurt drink)

=Vata @room temperature. -Pitta. +Kapha

½ cup plain yogurt

1½ cup water

½ cup sweet mango slices

Pinch of green cardamom powder

Few strands of saffron (if using)

- In a blender, blend all ingredients. Pour in a glass. Serve or cool a little.

Serves 1

Sizzling Soups around the world

We enjoy these soups as a full meal. These are chunky, nutritious, and each is packed with many servings of vegetables. I serve these with a piece of bread, paratha, a side of tofu, a quick greens stir fry, or whatever I need to make a complete meal.

Please also look for Middle Eastern soups under "Middle Eastern" section.

Butternut Squash Soup with Red Lentil Base

-Vata. =Pitta. +Kapha

¾ cup red lentils (red Masoor in Hindi)

3 cups butternut squash, peeled, seeded and cubed

1 cup carrots, diced or cubed

1 cup garbanzo beans cooked

1 large yellow onion chopped

1 inch ginger minced

2-3 cloves garlic minced

¼ -½ minced Thai or Indian green chili to taste

1 teaspoon turmeric

1½ teaspoon curry powder

Few sprigs fresh thyme leaves (stems removed)

Oil of your choice (that has high smoke-point)

Salt to taste

Freshly grounded black pepper to taste

2 teaspoons potato starch or any other thickener

- Wash lentils. Soak lentils in 4 cups of water for at least half an hour. Boil lentils until they are soft and mushy (add more water if needed).

- In a deep stew or soup pot, heat 3-4 tablespoon of oil.

- Add ginger, garlic and green chili and sauté until ginger and garlic turn light brown.

- Add onions. Sautee onions until they are light brown, about 7-8 minutes.

- Add curry powder and turmeric and sauté for a minute (can add more oil if needed).

- Add boiled lentils, butternut squash, carrots, salt, thyme leaves and 4 cups of water and bring it to a boil. Set heat to medium-low and cook for 30 minutes. (can add more water if needed).

- Add boiled garbanzo and freshly grounded black pepper.

- Dissolve 2 teaspoons of potato starch in ¼ cup of cold water.

- Pour potato starch liquid in pot slowly and keep stirring well. (can add more for thicker consistency). Cook for 5 minutes.

- Serve with some fresh thyme leaves as garnish.

Serves 6

Butternut Squash Soup with Carrots and Celery

-Vata. +Pitta. Slightly+Kapha

3 cups butternut squash, peeled, seeded and cubed

1 cup carrots, diced or cubed

1 cup celery, diced

1 large yellow onion chopped

1½ inch ginger minced

3-4 cloves garlic minced

6 cups vegetable broth

1 teaspoon turmeric

1 teaspoon curry powder (optional)

Few sprigs fresh thyme leaves (stems removed). Reserve little for garnish

5-6 sage leaves

Oil of your choice (that has high smoke-point)

Salt to taste

Freshly grounded black pepper to taste

Dash of cayenne pepper to taste (optional)

3 teaspoons potato starch or any other thickener

- In a deep stew or soup pot, heat 3-4 tablespoons of ghee or oil.

- Add ginger and garlic and sauté until ginger and garlic turn light brown.

- Add onions. Sautee onions until they are light brown, about 7-8 minutes.

- Add turmeric and curry powder (if using) and sauté in oil for about a minute.

- Add butternut squash, carrots, celery, broth, salt, thyme leaves, sage leaves and cook for about 30 minutes.

- Add freshly grounded black pepper and cayenne pepper if using.

- Dissolve 3 teaspoons of potato starch in ¼ cup of cold water.

- Pour potato starch liquid in pot slowly and keep stirring well. (can add more for thicker consistency). Cook for 5 more minutes.

- Adjust salt and black pepper if needed.

- Garnish with fresh thyme leaves.

Serves 6

Roasted Red Peppers and Garbanzo Soup

-Vata. Slightly+Pitta. +Kapha

4 large red bell peppers, cut in half and seeded

1 cup garbanzo beans cooked

2 large red onions chopped

6 large juicy Roma tomatoes

2 inch ginger minced

4 cloves garlic minced

¼ -½ minced Thai or Indian green chili to taste

Few sprigs fresh rosemary (stems removed)

Oil of your choice (that has high smoke-point)

Salt to taste

Freshly grounded black pepper to taste

½ cup (approx) Italian parsley chopped

- Roast peppers at 400F for about 40 minutes, turning once so both sides turn brownish.

- To make fresh tomato broth: puree 6 ripe and juicy Roma tomatoes in a blender. Add water to make it 4 cups.

- In a deep stew or soup pot, heat 2-3 tablespoons of oil.

- Add ginger, garlic and green chili and sauté until ginger and garlic turn light brown.

- Add onions. Sautee onions until they are light brown, about 6-7 minutes.

- While onions are cooking, puree 3 roasted red peppers in a food processor or blender.

- Cut 4th bell pepper into 1" squares.

- Add tomato broth, red pepper puree, salt, red pepper squares and rosemary to the pot and cook for 40 minutes.

- Add boiled garbanzo and freshly grounded black pepper. Cook for another 2-3 minutes.

- Ladle soup in soup bowls. Mix in generous amount of parsley in each bowl.

Serves 4

Vegetable Stew with Millet

Almost any vegetable or grain can be added to this stew. Play with other vegetables like squashes, zucchini, broccoli and varieties of potatoes.

-Vata. =Pitta. +Kapha

½ cup millet

1 cup potatoes cubed

1 cup carrots cubed

1 cup green beans cut in 2"

1 red or yellow onion chopped

8 Roma or wine-ripped tomatoes, pureed

1 cup frozen green peas

1 cup shelled edemame

1 cup cooked garbanzo

4 cloves garlic, minced or grated

2" ginger, minced or grated

1 teaspoon coriander powder

1 teaspoon dried mixed Italian herbs (or any other herbs you like)

1 teaspoon dried thyme leaves

Juice of 1 small lime

½ cup fresh parsley Italian chopped

Oil of your choice (that has high smoke-point)

Salt to taste

Freshly grounded black pepper to taste

- Puree tomatoes in a blender. Add water to make it 6 cups.

- In a deep stew or soup pot, heat 2-3 tablespoons of oil.

- Add onions. Sautee onions until they are translucent, about 6-7 minutes.

- Add ginger, garlic and sauté until all turn light brown.

- Add about 1 teaspoon of oil to one side of pot and add coriander powder to heated oil. Let it simmer for about 1 minute. Then mix everything.

- Add potatoes, carrots, tomato puree, millet, salt, thyme, other herbs and cook for 30 minutes.

- Add green beans, green peas, garbanzo, edemame, and cook for 10 more minutes.

- Close heat. Ladle in bowls. Add freshly grounded black pepper, lime and fresh parsley.

Serves 6

Cannellini Soup with Spinach and Barley

slightly+Vata. =Pitta. =Kapha

1 bunch spinach, washed and coarsely chopped (baby spinach is fine)

1 med yellow onion chopped

2 cups tomatoes diced

2 large red bell-peepers seeded and diced

½ cup barley

1½ inch ginger minced

6 cloves garlic minced

4 cups vegetable broth

2 cans cannellini beans rinsed

Few sprigs fresh rosemary (stems removed). Reserve little for garnish

1 teaspoon mixed Italian herbs

¼ teaspoon cayenne pepper

1 teaspoon curry powder

Oil of your choice (that has high smoke-point)

Salt to taste

Freshly grounded black pepper to taste

3 cups water

- Soak barley in one cup water for 2 hours.

- In a deep stew or soup pot, heat 3-4 tablespoons of oil.

- Add onions. Sautee onions until they are slightly darker (about 7-8 minutes on medium heat).

- While onions are cooking, grease a baking sheet and spread red bell peppers evenly. Adjust rack height to middle and broil peppers for 10 minutes. Close heat and let peppers sit in oven.

- Add ginger and garlic to the soup pot and sauté for 30 seconds. Add Italian herbs and mix well.

- Move everything to a side and add 1 teaspoon oil (preferably ghee if you have some) to the empty corner of the pot. Now add curry powder and cook in oil or ghee for at least 1 minute, constantly stirring it.

- Now mix all contents of pot well.

- Add tomatoes, vegetable broth, salt, drained barley, 3 cups water, and rosemary. Stir it.

- Bring it to a boil over high-heat. Reduce heat to medium. Cover. Cook for 45 minutes or until barley is tender.

- Add beans, red peppers, freshly grounded black pepper, cayenne pepper and cook for additional 5 minutes.

- Add spinach and cook for 2 minutes.

- Turn off heat. Ladle soup in bowls. Garnish with fresh rosemary leaves.

Serves 6-8

Tomatoes and Kidney-Beans soup with Mushrooms

This soup is laden with immunity boosting shitake and maitake mushrooms. Fresh and juicy tomatoes make the base. This soup is great for winter season.

slightly+Vata. +Pitta. +Kapha

1 15-oz red kidney beans can rinsed

2 cups fully-ripe Roma tomatoes pureed

1 large red or yellow onion chopped

1 large Yukon gold potato peeled and diced (can replace with sweet potato if you prefer a sweet taste)

1 large red bell-pepper diced

2 cups shitake or maitake mushrooms (replace with any mushrooms if those are not available)

1 inch ginger minced

4 cloves garlic minced

¼ - ½ jalapeno seeded and finely chopped

4 cups vegetable broth

4 sage leaves

1 teaspoon cumin powder

Dash of cayenne pepper

2 tablespoon dried thyme leaves

Oil of your choice (that has high smoke-point)

Salt to taste

1 cup Italian parsley chopped (optional)

- In a deep stew or soup pot, heat 5-6 tablespoons of oil.

- Add ginger, garlic and jalapeno and sauté until ginger and garlic turn light brown.

- Add onions. Sautee onions until they change color, about 8-9 minutes.

- Add cumin powder and sauté for 30 seconds.

- Add mushrooms and potatoes and sauté for 3-4 minutes.

- Add pureed tomatoes, broth, red bell pepper, salt, sage leaves, thyme leaves and bring it to a boil.

- Reduce heat to low and cook for 40 minutes. (You can boil potatoes separately if you wish to reduce cooking time).

- Add red kidney beans and cayenne. Cook for 4-5 minutes.

- Ladle soup in bowls. Mix in fresh parsley.
Serves 6

White Bean soup with Kale

slightly+Vata. =Pitta. =Kapha

1 large bunch Kale (can use red chard instead of Kale) washed, dried, veins /stems removed and coarsely chopped).

1 large red or yellow onion chopped

1 cup carrots diced

1 cup celery diced

1½ inch ginger minced

4 cloves garlic minced

1 green chili minced

4 cups vegetable broth

1 15-oz can cannellini beans, rinsed

Few sprigs fresh rosemary (stems removed). Reserve little for garnish

5-6 sage leaves

Ghee or oil of your choice (that has high smoke-point)

Salt to taste

Freshly grounded black pepper to taste

3-4 teaspoons potato starch or any other thickener

- In a deep stew or soup pot, heat 3-4 tablespoons of ghee or oil.

- Add ginger, garlic and chili and sauté until ginger and garlic turn light brown.

- Add onions. Sautee onions until they are light brown, about 7-8 minutes.

- Add carrots, celery, broth, salt, rosemary leaves, sage leaves and cook for about 20 minutes.

- Add beans and freshly grounded black pepper.

- Dissolve 3 teaspoons of potato starch in ¼ cup of cold water. Pour potato starch liquid in pot slowly and keep stirring well. (add more for thicker consistency).

- Add kale or chard leaves and cook for 5 minutes (adjust more or less time depending on how cooked you like your greens).

- Garnish with fresh rosemary leaves.

Serves 4

Pumpkin Soup

-Vata. =Pitta. slightly+Kapha

3 cups pumpkin (big pieces OK)

1 cup carrots (big pieces OK)

1 cup celery (big pieces OK)

2 leeks coarsely sliced

1½ inch ginger minced

4 cloves garlic minced

½ -1 minced Thai or Indian green chili to taste

½ teaspoon turmeric

¼ teaspoon cinnamon

¼ teaspoon nutmeg

Dash of cayenne pepper to taste (optional)

5 cups water

Oil of your choice (that has high smoke-point)

Salt to taste

Freshly grounded black pepper to taste

Few leaves of fresh thyme, oregano or herb of your choice

- Grease a baking sheet. Bake pumpkin and carrots at 400F for 25-30 minutes. Close heat. Let it sit in oven for another 10 minutes.

- In a deep stew or soup pot, heat 3-4 tablespoons of ghee or oil.

- Add ginger, garlic and chili and sauté until ginger and garlic turn light brown.

- Add leeks. Sautee leeks until they become translucent.

- Add turmeric and sauté in oil for about a minute (can add more oil now).

- Add cinnamon and nutmeg powder and cook for few seconds.

- Add celery and cook it for 1-2 minutes.

- Add pumpkin, carrots, salt and water. Using an immersion blender, blend everything well.

- Cook for 15-20 minutes constantly stirring.

- Add freshly grounded black pepper and cayenne pepper if using.

- Take off heat. Ladle hot soup in bowl. Garnish with any herb of your choice. Mine is usually thyme.

Serves 6

Potato Leek Corn soup

My husband LOVES this soup (although I make so many other soups far more delicious than this one), so I make this soup very often in winter.

-Vata. +Pitta. +Kapha

3 cups Yukon gold potatoes peeled and ½" cubed

1 cup carrots diced

1 cup celery diced

2 leeks thinly sliced

1 cup frozen organic sweet corn

1½ inch ginger minced

4-5 cloves garlic minced

4 cups vegetable broth

Few sprigs fresh rosemary leaves (stems removed). Reserve little for garnish

5-6 sage leaves

Oil of your choice (that has high smoke-point)

Salt to taste

Freshly grounded black pepper to taste

Dash of cayenne pepper

3-4 teaspoons potato starch or any other thickener

2 sprigs chives thinly sliced

- In a deep stew or soup pot, heat 3-4 tablespoons of oil.

- Add ginger and garlic and sauté until ginger and garlic turn light brown.

- Add onions. Sautee leeks until they soften, about 4-5 minutes.

- Add potatoes, carrots and celery and sauté for 2-3 minutes.

- Add broth, salt, rosemary leaves, sage leaves and cook for about 25-30 minutes.

- Add freshly grounded black pepper, cayenne pepper and sweet corn to the pot.

- Dissolve 3 teaspoons of potato starch in ¼ cup of cold water.

- Pour potato starch liquid in pot slowly and keep stirring well. (Add more for thicker consistency). Cook for 5 more minutes, stirring few times.

- Adjust salt and black pepper if needed.

- Garnish with reserved fresh rosemary leaves and chives.

Serves 4

Coconut Curry Soup with Potatoes, Garbanzo and Kale

slightly+Vata. -Pitta. +Kapha

1 large yellow onion chopped

2 cups celery diced

1 cup potatoes cubed

2 cups tomatoes chopped

2 cups carrots diced

1 15-oz can light coconut milk

1 bunch kale, coarsely chopped

4 cups vegetable broth

1 15oz can garbanzos beans rinsed

1 inch fresh ginger grated or chopped

4 cloves garlic grated or chopped

¼ -½ Thai or Indian green chili

1 teaspoon cumin powder

1 teaspoon curry powder

½ teaspoon cinnamon

¼ teaspoon nutmeg powder

¼ teaspoon cayenne pepper powder

Rice bran oil

Salt to taste

Juice of 1 - 1½ large lime

1 - 2 teaspoons potato starch or any other thickener (optional)

1 cup water

- In a deep stew or soup pot, heat 3-4 tablespoons of rice bran oil.

- Add onions. Sautee onions until they are light brown, about 7-8 minutes.

- Add ginger and garlic and sauté for 1-2 minutes.

- Add cumin powder and curry powder and cook for 1 minute.

- Add tomatoes, vegetable broth, coconut milk, celery, potatoes, carrots, 1 cup water and salt. Stir.

- Bring it to boil, reduce heat and simmer for 15 minutes or until potatoes are almost tender.

- Add garbanzo beans, cinnamon, nutmeg, cayenne pepper and cook for 5 minutes.

- Add Kale and lime juice and cook for 4 minutes. Adjust spices if needed.

- Dissolve 1 teaspoon of potato starch in ¼ cup of cold water. Pour potato starch liquid in pot slowly and keep stirring well. Repeat this if you like it thicker. (if you like your soup thinner, you do not have to add any starch).

- Take off heat immediately. Serve hot.

Serves 8

Healthy Foods and International Recipes balanced Ayurvedically

I live in California. Oh, yes! You can catch few farmers markets in a week. Fresh kale, Swiss chard, collard greens, spinach, broccoli, broccolini, mustard greens, basil, cilantro, parsley, all kinds of berries, varieties and colors of juicy stone fruits, many species of tomatoes, colorful carrots and beets, persimmons, pomegranates, every imaginable variety of citrus fruits and…. so much to play with, in your kitchen…..

And then there is quinoa, wild-rice, alternative grains, tofu, tempeh, miso, raw, gluten-free, vegan, smoothies, fresh juices, every kind of hummus and ……. all these have invaded family kitchens, health markets, fancy restaurants and cafes alike.

In this section, I use nature's fresh and seasonal bounty, different greens, salads/raw food, and western recipes that I love. Since I love to eat these foods and most are not Ayurvedically balanced, I altered and improvised them to minimally sautéed or cooked (instead of raw), and made them easily digestible using ginger, garlic, garam masala, curry powder, turmeric, sesame seeds, black pepper, tamari, soy sauce, western spices and green herbs like sage, basil, cilantro, parsley, thyme, oregano, mint etc.

Kale Sauté with Ginger and Almonds

If someone told me few years ago that I would be stealing this kale from my husband's plate after finishing my share, I would have had a real hard laugh. I have come to love this kale so much. Every time I teach this recipe, I have proudly converted people to kale lovers.

+Vata. =Pitta. −Kapha

1 large bunch Dino kale, washed, dried, stem removed and coarsely chopped

2 inch ginger minced or grated

3 tablespoons almond slices

Oil of your choice for sautéing

Himalayan pink salt to taste

Lime

Freshly grounded black pepper to taste

- Heat 3-4 tablespoons oil in a wok or frying pan.

- On low heat, add ginger and almond slices and sauté until ginger turns light brown (you can also dry-toast almond slices separately).

- Add kale and mix everything well. Keep turning kale so it does not stick to pan. Cook for 5-7 minutes (depends on how crunchy and fresh you like it).

- Take off the heat. Sprinkle with lime, salt and freshly grounded black pepper.

Serves 2

Try other variations:

- Sprinkle grounded flax seeds or hemp seeds.

- Add black sesame seeds or white sesame seeds.

- Play with your favorite nuts.

Swiss chard Sauté with sesame

+Vata. =Pitta. −Kapha

1 large bunch Swiss chard, washed, dried, veins removed, and coarsely chopped

2 inch ginger minced or grated

1 tablespoon white sesame seeds

1 tablespoon black sesame seeds

Any nuts or seeds of your choice (optional)

1 tablespoon hemp seeds

Oil of your choice for sautéing

Himalayan pink salt to taste

Freshly grounded black pepper to taste (optional)

- Heat 2-3 tablespoons oil in a wok or frying pan on very low heat.

- Add ginger and sesame seeds together. Sauté until ginger turns light golden.

- Add Swiss chard and sauté for about 2-3 minutes (Swiss chard loses most of its volume quickly).

- Take off the heat immediately. Sprinkle with salt, freshly grounded black pepper and hemp seeds.

- Add nuts or seeds if using.

Serves 1

Collard Greens Sauté

+Vata. +Pitta. −Kapha

1 large bunch collard greens, washed, dried, veins removed, and coarsely chopped

1 inch ginger grated or minced

2 cloves garlic grated or minced

Juice of half orange

Juice of half lime

1 teaspoon honey

Oil of your choice for sautéing

Himalayan pink salt to taste

Freshly grounded black pepper to taste

- Heat 3-4 tablespoons oil in a wok or frying pan on very low heat.

- Add ginger and garlic. Sauté until light golden.

- Add collard greens. Sauté for 3-5 minutes.

- Take off the heat immediately.

- In a bowl, mix orange juice, lime juice, honey, salt and black pepper.

- Pour dressing on collard greens and toss. Serves 2

Brussels sprouts Sauté

+Vata. =Pitta. −Kapha

2 cups Brussels sprouts sliced in half length-wise (cut hard bottoms)

1 inch ginger minced or grated

Few sprigs rosemary leaves removed

Oil of your choice for sautéing

Himalayan pink salt to taste

Lime to taste

Freshly grounded black pepper to taste

- Heat 3 tablespoons oil in a wok or frying pan on very low heat.

- Add ginger and sauté until ginger starts to change color. Do not over-cook.

- Add Brussels sprouts and mix. After few minutes, turn Brussels sprouts to cook on other side.

- When second side is almost done, add rosemary. Mix everything well and sauté for another 1-2 minutes.

- Take off the heat. Sprinkle with lime, salt and freshly grounded black pepper and mix   thoroughly.
  Serves 2

Broccolini or Baby Broccoli Sauté

slightly+Vata. -Pitta. —Kapha

1 bunch broccolini or baby broccoli cut in 2 inch longs

2 inch ginger minced or grated

1 tablespoon white sesame seeds

1 tablespoon black sesame seeds

Oil of your choice for Sautéing

1 tablespoon toasted black sesame oil for dressing (optional)

Himalayan pink salt to taste

Freshly grounded black pepper to taste

Juice of ½ small lime

- Heat 3-4 tablespoons oil in a wok or frying pan on very low heat.

- Add ginger and sesame seeds together. Sauté for about 1 minute.

- Add broccolini or baby broccoli and sauté it for about 4-5 minutes constantly turning it.

- Take off the heat immediately. Sprinkle with salt, freshly grounded black pepper and lime juice and mix well.

- Sprinkle toasted black sesame if using. Serve immediately.

Serves 1

Try other variation:

-Instead of black sesame oil, sprinkle 1-2 tablespoon nutritional yeast to add a cheesy flavor.

Summer Quinoa Salad

=Vata. Slightly+Pitta. −Kapha

1 cup quinoa

1 cup cherry or grape tomatoes halved

1 cup boiled sweet corn

1 cup celery cut in small pieces

½ cup green onions chopped

1 cup cilantro chopped

Olive oil (optional)

Himalayan pink salt to taste

Freshly grounded black pepper to taste

Juice of 1 lemon or lime

- Wash quinoa. Boil it in 1.5 cups of water. When water starts to evaporate, reduce heat to low. Quinoa should be cooked and dry. Set aside and let it cool.

- Wash and cut all vegetables while quinoa is boiling.

- In a large mixing bowl, mix all ingredients very well.

- Fluff boiled quinoa with a fork and add to the mixing bowl. Drizzle with little olive oil (optional) and mix well.

- Adjust salt, black pepper, lemon (or lime) to taste.

Serves 2

Try other variations:

- ½ cup fresh chopped basil instead of cilantro.

- In winter, grate or finely chop small piece (about 1 inch) piece of ginger. Sauté ginger in oil on low heat until it turns golden. Add ginger to the salad. Or try adding little garlic along ginger.

- In summer, try adding other veggies like raw cucumbers, red and colored bell peppers etc.

Quinoa with Kale and Garbanzo

+Vata. +Pitta. =Kapha

1 cup quinoa

1 cup cherry or grape tomatoes cut in 4s

2 cups boiled garbanzo beans

2-3 cups (packed) kale leaves, (washed, dried, stem removed and coarsely chopped)

1 cup cucumbers diced

1 inch ginger chopped

2 tablespoons tamari sauce

2-3 tablespoons olive oil

1 teaspoon honey

Juice of 1 lime

2 tablespoons any oil of your choice for sautéing

Himalayan pink salt to taste

Freshly grounded black pepper to taste

¼ cup roasted sunflower seeds (optional)

- Wash quinoa. Boil it in 1.5 cups of water. When water starts to evaporate, reduce heat to low. Quinoa should be cooked and dry. Set aside and let it cool.

- Heat 2 tablespoons of oil on low heat. Add ginger and sauté ginger slowly. When ginger turns light brown, add kale to it and sauté for 5-7 minutes on low heat. DO NOT over-cook kale. Let it cool for few minutes.

- In a large mixing bowl, add tomatoes, garbanzos, cucumbers, sautéed ginger and kale.

- Fluff boiled quinoa with a fork and add to the mixing bowl.

- In a small bowl, mix olive oil, tamari sauce, honey, lime juice, freshly grounded black pepper and mix very well. Taste before adding salt as tamari already has salt.

- Adjust salt, black pepper, lime and tamari to taste.

Serves 2 as main dish. Serves 4 as side dish or salad.

Quinoa with Butternut Squash and Kale

I taught this recipe in one of my cooking workshop. I have never received so much praise and emails. Everyone just loved this combination.

+Vata. +Pitta. −Kapha

I bunch kale, washed, dried, stem removed and coarsely chopped

1 cup quinoa

3 cups butternut squash diced 1" cubes (may use any other squash or sweet potatoes instead)

2 tablespoons slivered almonds

4 tablespoons any oil of your choice

1 inch ginger grated or chopped

½ - 1 cup basil cut in ribbons for garnish

Dressing:

4 tablespoons lime or lemon juice

2 tablespoon roasted sesame oil (can use olive oil instead)

2 teaspoons honey

1 teaspoon tamari

Juice of 1 large orange

Himalayan pink salt to taste

Freshly grounded black pepper to taste

- Preheat oven to 400F. Oil a baking sheet and spread squash evenly. Bake Squash for about 20 minutes or until soft, turning once or twice so it is evenly cooked.

- Wash quinoa. Boil it in 1.5 cups of water. When water starts to evaporate, reduce heat to low. Quinoa should be cooked and dry. Set aside and let it cool.

- Heat 2 tablespoons of oil on low heat. Add ginger and almonds and sauté. When ginger turns light brown, add kale to it and sauté for 5-7 minutes on low heat. DO NOT over-cook kale. Fluff boiled quinoa with a fork. Let it cool for few minutes.

- In a large mixing bowl, add squash, sautéed almonds, ginger, kale and quinoa.

- In a small bowl, whisk together all dressing ingredients.

- Drizzle everything with dressing and mix very well.

- Adjust salt and pepper. If it feels dry, you can squeeze more orange juice over quinoa and mix again.

- Garnish with basil ribbons.

Serves 2

Summer Cashew Cranberry Quinoa

+Vata. =Pitta. Slightly+Kapha

1 cup quinoa

½ cup roasted cashews (cashew pieces are OK)

½ cup dried cranberries

1 cup parsley chopped

½ cup green onions chopped (green part only)

¼ cup mint chopped

1 inch ginger chopped

1 tablespoon sautéing oil

Himalayan pink salt to taste

Freshly grounded black pepper to taste

Juice of 2 large limes

1-2 tablespoon olive oil or avocado Oil

1 teaspoon grounded flax seeds or hemp seeds (optional)

- Wash quinoa. Boil it in 1.5 cups of water. When water starts to evaporate, reduce heat to low. Quinoa should be cooked and dry. Set aside and let it cool.

- Wash and cut all greens while quinoa is boiling.

- In a small pan, add 1 Tablespoon sautéing oil of your choice. Sauté ginger on low heat for about 2-3 minutes until it is slight brown. Take off heat.

- Fluff boiled quinoa with a fork and place in a large mixing bowl.

- Add all other ingredients and sautéed ginger. Drizzle with olive or avocado oil, lime juice and mix everything well.

- Adjust salt, black pepper and lime to taste.

- Place in bowl. Sprinkle grounded flax seeds or hemp seeds in the bowl (optional).

Serves 4

Garbanzo and Kale in Roasted Red Pepper Sauce

+Vata. +Pitta. =Kapha

I large bunch Dino kale, washed, dried, stem removed and coarsely chopped

1 15-oz garbanzo can

2 large red peppers cleaned

1 large green pepper cleaned

1 large yellow or orange pepper cleaned

3 stalks celery 1" diced

1 cup green onions thinly sliced (both white and green parts)

2 cloves garlic (1 whole and 1 chopped)

2 inch ginger grated or chopped

4 tablespoons oil of your choice for sautéing

4 tablespoon fresh thyme leaves

¼ cup lime juice

Himalayan pink salt to taste

Freshly grounded black pepper to taste

5-6 Tablespoon olive or avocado oil for sauce

Dash of cayenne pepper or ¼ fresh Serrano chili seeded (optional)

- Oil a baking sheet. Cut 1 red bell pepper, 1 green bell pepper, 1 orange (or yellow) pepper into 1" cubes and spread on baking sheet. Cut second red bell pepper into 8 or 10 long stripes and spread on baking sheet. Set the baking tray to medium rack. Broil for 15 minutes, turning peppers twice.

- In a wide pan, heat 4 tablespoons of sautéing oil on low heat. Add ginger and 1 chopped clove of garlic and sauté for about 1 minute.

- Add green onions and sauté for about 2-3 minutes.

- Add kale and sauté for about 4-5 minutes. DO NOT over-cook kale. Take off heat and let it cool for few minutes. Once cooled, transfer it to a large mixing bowl.

- Place green and red bell pepper cubes, celery and garbanzo in the mixing bowl.

- In a blender or chopper, blend long stripes of broiled red pepper, olive or avocado oil, salt, black pepper, lime juice, half of thyme leaves, 1 clove garlic, and cayenne pepper or ¼ Serrano chili (if using).

- Pour the sauce on veggies in the bowl. Add remaining thyme leaves to the bowl and mix everything well.

- Adjust salt, black pepper, lime and thyme if needed.

Serves 2 as main dish. Serves 4 as salad or side dish.

Summer Kale salad with Carrots, Red Peppers and Golden Beets

+Vata. +Pitta. −Kapha

1 large curly kale bunch (washed, dried, stem removed and cut in ribbons)

2 cups red bell peppers cut in stripes

2 cups carrots grated

1 cup golden beets grated (grate these last as they oxidize very fast)

3-4 tablespoons hemp seeds

2 tablespoons dried thyme leaves

2-3 tablespoons any oil of your choice for kale

Himalayan pink salt to taste

Freshly grounded black pepper to taste

Nutritional yeast (optional)

Dressing:

2 tablespoons tamari sauce

4 tablespoons olive or avocado oil

5 tablespoons apple cider vinegar

3 teaspoons Tahini

- Heat 2-3 tablespoons of oil of your choice on low heat. Add kale to it and sauté for 1-2 minutes on low heat. Turn and cook for another minute. Take off heat immediately. Let it cool for few minutes.

- In a large mixing bowl, place kale and all vegetables.

- In a medium bowl, pour all dressing ingredients and mix very well.

- Pour dressing over salad. Sprinkle thyme, salt, black pepper, hemp seeds and toss everything well. Serve immediately.

- Serve with nutritional yeast (optional) if any one likes to add a cheesy and creamier taste.

Serves 6

Millet Pilaf with Beans & Greens

+Vata. +Pitta. =Kapha

1 cup millet

1 cup boiled black or kidney beans or garbanzo

½ cup red onions finely chopped

1 red bell pepper chopped

½ cup green onions chopped

1 cup cilantro chopped

½ cup parsley chopped

1 teaspoon cumin grounded

Oil of your choice

Himalayan pink salt to taste

Freshly grounded black pepper to taste

Juice of 1 lemon or lime

- Wash millet. Boil it in 2 cups of water.
- Wash and cut all vegetables while millet is boiling.

- Boil millet until all water is evaporated. Set aside to cool.

- In a wok or large pan, sauté red onions in olive oil.

- When onions are translucent, add grounded cumin and sauté well for about 1 minute. Remove from heat.

- Add rest of the ingredients and mix well.

- Fluff millet with a fork and add. Mix well.

- Adjust salt, black pepper, lemon (or lime) to the taste.

Serves 2

Try other variations:

- Chopped fresh mint

- Different varieties of beans/garbanzo

- Cherry tomatoes

Wild Rice and Squash Sautee with Creamy Sunflower Dressing

-Vata. +Pitta. +Kapha

3 cups any winter squash (I love butternut squash)

1 cup wild rice

2 medium yellow onions chopped length wise

1½ inch ginger

Oil of your choice

2 cups Italian parsley finely chopped

Dressing:

1/6 cup sunflower seeds

4 tablespoons lemon or lime juice

1 tablespoon honey

4 tablespoons water

1 tablespoon olive oil

Himalayan pink salt to taste

Freshly grounded black pepper to taste

- Preheat oven to 400F. Oil a baking sheet and spread squash evenly. Bake Squash for about 20 minutes or until soft, turning once or twice so it is evenly cooked.

- Rinse wild rice. Cook in 2½ cups of water for 50 minute to an hour (depends on how firm you like your rice). Set aside.

- In a medium frying pan, heat oil on low. Add onions and sauté very slowly until onions are caramelized, turning constantly.

- Add ginger to the pan and sauté for about 2-3 more minutes. Take off heat.

- In a blender or food processor, puree dressing ingredients. You can add more water if you prefer a thinner consistency. Adjust salt and lime (or lemon).

- Place rice, squash, and sautéed onion/ginger in a large bowl. Toss with dressing and mix well. Adjust salt and black pepper if needed.

- Mix in parsley before serving.

Serves 4

Wild Rice and Lima Beans with fresh veggies

+Vata. +Pitta. −Kapha

1½ cups lima beans

1 cup wild rice

2 cups red bell peppers chopped

2 cups celery chopped

2 cups Italian parsley finely chopped

½ cup green onions chopped (only greens) (optional)

Freshly grounded black pepper to taste

Dressing:

¼ cup Lime juice

4 tablespoons olive oil

2 tablespoons honey

2 cloves garlic peeled

1 inch ginger peeled

Juice of ½ orange

1 tablespoon balsamic or red wine or apple cider vinegar (optional)

Himalayan pink salt to taste

- Pre-soak Lima beans over-night. Boil in a covered pan for about 40-50 minutes on medium heat. Discard any remaining water. Let it cool.

- Rinse wild rice. Cook in 2½ cups of water for 50 minute to an hour (depends on how firm you like your rice). Set aside.

- In a blender or food processor, puree dressing ingredients. Adjust salt and lime.

- In a large mixing bowl, add lima beans, wild rice and all veggies.

- Toss gently with dressing and freshly grounded black pepper.

Serves 6

Baked Root Vegetables

-Vata. =Pitta. +Kapha

2 cups Yukon gold potatoes peeled and cubed

2 cups sweet potatoes or garnet yams peeled and cubed

2 cups carrots, peeled, sliced or cubed

1 cup beets, peeled, cubed

Any other root vegetable you like

1 red onion 1" cubed

2 cups green bell pepper 1"cubed

2 inch ginger grated or finely chopped

4 cloves garlic minced

Few sprigs of fresh rosemary stems removed (reserve some for garnish)

¼ teaspoon garam masala powder (optional)

High-smoke point oil (like rice bran oil)

Himalayan pink salt to taste

Freshly grounded black pepper to taste

- Preheat oven to 400F. Oil a baking sheet generously and spread all root vegetables. Toss some oil, salt, black pepper, generous amount of rosemary and mix it all well. Bake for about 40 minutes or until roots are soft, turning once or twice so roots are evenly cooked.

- While roots are baking, heat 4-5 tablespoons of oil on low heat. Add ginger and sauté ginger slowly. When ginger turns light brown, add onions and sauté until onions become light brownish (7-8 minutes).

- Add garam masala powder is using. Mix well and cook for about 30 seconds-1 minute.

- Add green bell peppers and cook for 4-5 minutes. DO NOT over-cook bell peppers.

- Close heat immediately. Add hot root vegetables. Toss in more fresh rosemary leaves. Adjust salt and black pepper.

Serves 4

Baked Tofu with Asian sauce

+Vata. +Pitta. =Kapha

1 box (15-16oz) extra firm organic tofu

Oil for oiling baking sheet

1 tablespoon white sesame seeds

1 tablespoon black sesame seeds

Sauce:

1 tablespoon tamari

3 tablespoons low-sodium soy sauce

½ teaspoon brown sugar

1 tablespoon grated/chopped ginger

2 cloves garlic

- In a food processor, chop ginger and garlic. Add tamari, soy sauce and sugar. Mix it few more seconds.

- Preheat oven to 400F.

- Oil a baking sheet.

- Squeeze extra water from tofu gently. Don't break the tofu.

- Cut tofu into long stripes of approx ½" of thickness. Spread on baking sheet.

- With a teaspoon, spread sauce evenly on each tofu stripe. Do not discard any sauce (I like to use extra sauce as a dipping sauce while eating my tofu).

- Sprinkle white and black sesame seeds on tofu generously.

- Set tray on middle rack. Bake tofu for 20-25 minutes (time depends on brand and firmness of tofu. Less firm tofu or one with extra water takes longer duration).

- Close heat but let tofu sit in oven for another 5-6 minutes.

- Enjoy it alone or with extra sauce as a dip.

Serves 4 as side dish.

Red Curry Lentils with spinach

Two of my favorite cuisines married in my kitchen and we loved it happily ever after; India meets Thailand. This recipe is quick and easy, so nourishing and comforting, and completely fool-proof.

-Vata. =Pitta. +Kapha

1 onion chopped

2 cups red lentils washed

2 cups tomatoes chopped

1 15-oz can light coconut milk

4 cups (packed) spinach leaves, coarsely chopped

4 cups vegetable broth

1 cup frozen green peas

1 cup carrots chopped

1 cup celery chopped (optional)

1 inch fresh ginger grated or chopped

3 cloves garlic minced or chopped

2 tablespoons Red curry paste (it is available at any health or conventional store these days)

1 teaspoon cumin powder

Juice of 2 limes

1 cup cilantro chopped for garnish

2 sprigs green onion sliced thin for garnish (greens only)

Rice bran oil

Himalayan pink salt to taste

Freshly grated black pepper to taste

- In a deep stew or soup pot, heat 3-4 tablespoons of rice bran oil.

- Add ginger and garlic and sauté for 1 minute.

- Add onions. Sautee onions until they are light brown, 6-7 minutes.

- While onions are cooking, dissolve red curry paste in coconut milk in a small bowl.

- Add cumin powder to pot and sauté for 30 seconds. Mix all well.

- Add lentils, tomatoes, vegetable broth, salt, coconut milk and 1 cup water. Mix everything well.

- Add carrots and celery.

- Bring it to boil, reduce heat and simmer for 15-20 minutes.

- While curry is cooking, wash and chop spinach.

- Add green peas, spinach, lime juice and freshly grounded black pepper and cook for 5-10 minutes (depending on how cooked you like your spinach).

- Adjust salt, pepper and lime to taste.

- Ladle in soup bowls. Garnish with fresh cilantro and green onions. Serve with white rice or brown rice or Chinese 8-grains rice.

Serves 6

Vegetarian Singapore Noodles

-Vata. +Pitta. —Kapha

5-6 oz thin vermicelli rice noodles

2 cups baby broccoli or broccolini cut into 2"longs

1 cup carrots cut in thin 2" longs

1 cup green onions sliced in middle and cut in 2" longs

2 cups green bell pepper cut in 2" longs

Baby bok choy, bottoms cut length-wise, leaves chopped in thick ribbons

½ box of Organic Extra-firm tofu (about 7-8oz) cut in 2" long / ½"wide slices

1 inch ginger finely chopped or grated

3 cloves garlic finely chopped or grated

Sauce:

2 tablespoons tamari

3 tablespoons low-sodium soy sauce

4 tablespoons rice vinegar

1 ½ - 2 teaspoons curry powder (depending you how strong and fresh your curry powder is)

½ teaspoon Siracha sauce (optional)

Rice bran oil for sautéing

Salt to taste (tamari/soy sauce already have salt)

Freshly grated black pepper to taste

- In a wok or wide pan, heat 5-6 tablespoons of oil. Add ginger and garlic and sauté for 30 seconds.

- Add green onions and sauté for 2 minutes. Add carrots to pan and sauté for another 5-6 minutes.

- While vegetables are cooking, mix all sauce ingredients well and keep aside.

- Add green bell peppers and broccoli to the pan and sauté for 3-4 minutes.

- While vegetables are sautéing, boil water in a deep pot. Add noodles and cook for 5-6 minutes (or as packet instructions). Strain noodles and let extra water drain out.

- Add bok choy to the vegetables pan and sauté for about 1 minute. Add tofu and mix slowly so you don't break the tofu.

- Turn heat to simmer. Add noodles. Pour sauce on noodles. Using two flat wooden turners toss and cover all vegetables & noodles with sauce. Taste and adjust salt, black pepper, vinegar and soy sauce if needed.

- Close lid and cook it for 1-2 minute. Take off heat right away and serve immediately. Serves 4

Asian Veggie Sauté

-Vata. +Pitta. —Kapha

1 medium yellow onion cut in long slices

1 ½ - 2 cups broccoli or baby broccoli cut into 2"longs

1 cup carrots cut in thin 2" longs

2-3 springs green onions sliced in middle and cut in 2" longs

1 cup celery cut in 2" longs

½ cup wood-year mushrooms sliced

½ cup shitake mushrooms sliced

Baby bok choy, bottoms sliced length-wise, leaves coarsely chopped in thick ribbons

½ box of organic Extra-firm tofu (about 7-8oz) cut in 2" long / ½"wide slices

2 inch ginger finely chopped or grated

8 cloves garlic finely chopped or grated

1 tablespoon black sesame seeds

3 tablespoons low-sodium soy sauce

2 tablespoons rice vinegar

½ - 1 teaspoon Schwezan sauce or 1 teaspoon Hoisin sauce (Schwezan sauce is hot. use Hoisin sauce if you do not like heat)

Toasted black sesame oil for sautéing

Freshly grated black pepper to taste

- In a wok or wide pan, heat 4-5 tablespoons of oil. Add ginger and garlic and sauté for about 1 minute.

- Add yellow onion and sauté for 4-5 minutes.

- Add carrots and mushrooms to the pan and sauté for 4-5 minutes.

- Add celery, broccoli and green onions to the pan and sauté for 3-4 minutes.

- Add Schwezan sauce and add tofu immediately. Sauté tofu in the sauce for few seconds.

- Turn heat to very low. Add bok choy to the pan and let it cook for about 1 minute or until it loses its volume.

- Add black sesame seeds, soy sauce, vinegar immediately and mix everything slowly so you don't break the tofu.

- Taste and adjust vinegar and soy sauce if needed.

- Take off heat and serve immediately.

Enjoy alone for a healthy meal or serve over brown jasmine rice or brown Basmati rice.

Serves 4

Indonesian Red Rice

-Vata. +Pitta. +Kapha

1 cup red rice

1 cup green beans cut in 1"

1 cup carrots sliced

6 large shallots sliced length-wise

1½ inch ginger grated or chopped

3 cloves garlic grated or chopped

1 cup light coconut milk

½ small green or red chili seeded and finely chopped

1 teaspoon coriander powder

1 teaspoon curry powder

1/6 cup low-sodium soy sauce

6 tablespoons rice bran oil

1 small fresh lime

Salt to taste

Freshly grounded black pepper to taste

1 small yellow onion, sliced length-wise

Toasted black sesame oil

1 cup fresh cilantro chopped

2 sprigs green onions thinly sliced (green part only)

- Wash Rice. Soak it in 2 cups water for about an hour. Bring it to a boil, then turn heat to low and cook rice until tender (about 30-35 minutes). Set aside.

- In a wok or large wide pan, heat 6 tablespoons of oil on medium-low heat. Add ginger, garlic, chili and sauté for 1 minute.

- Add shallots and sauté for 4 minutes.

- Add green beans and carrots and cook until veggies are half-cooked. They should be crisp (about 5-6 minutes).

- While veggies are coking, heat toasted sesame oil in a separate frying pan. Add yellow onions in oil. Cook until onions turn crispy. Set aside.

- In main veggies pan, add coriander and curry powder. Mix well and cook for 1 minute.

- Add soy sauce, coconut milk, juice of 1 small fresh lime, salt, black pepper and mix well. Bring it to a boil.

- Turn heat to very low. Add rice. Toss and mix everything well. Adjust salt and pepper if needed. Take off heat immediately.

- Plate Rice. Top it with generous amount of cilantro, crispy yellow onions and green onions. Can add more lime now if needed.

Serves 2

Purple Yam Asian Rice

-Vata. -Pitta. +Kapha

1 cup 8-grain Asian rice (available at Asian grocery stores)

2 medium purple yams peeled and cubed (available at Asian grocery stores)

1 tablespoon ghee

4 sprigs green onions sliced thin (green part only)

1 yellow onion chopped length-wise

2-3 tablespoons rice bran oil or oil of your choice

Himalayan pink salt to taste

Freshly grounded black pepper to taste

2 sprigs green onions thinly sliced (green part only)

- Wash Rice. Soak it in 3 cups water for about 2 hours. Bring it to a boil. Turn heat to low.

- Add yams, ghee, salt, black pepper and cook until rice is tender, about 35-40 minutes.

- While rice is cooking, heat rice bran oil in a frying pan. Add yellow onions and fry until they are crisp. Drain out extra oil. Set aside. (avoid this step to make the dish low-fat and healthier version)

- Plate hot rice. Layer fried onions at top of rice.

- Garnish generously with raw green onions.

Serves 4

Potatoes, Fennel and Peppers Sauté

A perfect blend of East and West, much like me.

-Vata. =Pitta. +Kapha

3 Yukon gold potatoes peeled and sliced length-wise in 1" stripes

1 yellow or Maui onion sliced length-wise

1 large green bell pepper cut lengthwise in 1" stripes

1 large red bell pepper cut lengthwise in 1" stripes

1 cup fresh fennel bulb shaved thick or thinly sliced. Separately chop green leaves for garnish

1 cup frozen green peas

1½ inch ginger chopped

3 cloves garlic chopped

1 tablespoon cumin seeds

High-heat oil of your choice

Himalayan pink salt to taste

Freshly grounded black pepper to taste

Pinch of garam masala (optional)

- Heat about 4-5 Tablespoon oil in a wide pan. Sauté potatoes until they are cooked. (Alternatively, you can bake potatoes).

- While potatoes are cooking, heat about 6 tablespoons oil in a separate wok or wide pan.

- Add cumin seeds. Cook until they start popping.

- Add minced ginger and garlic. Stir 30 second, add onions. Sauté for about 5-7 minutes.

- Add peppers. Cover. Cook for 5 minutes, constantly turning.

- Add cooked potatoes, green peas and fennel. Sprinkle with salt, black pepper and garam masala (if using). Mix everything well slowly. Can add more oil if needed.

- Cook for another 5 minutes or until all veggies are soft but not mushy.

- Take off heat. Garnish with chopped fennel leaves.

Serves 4

Middle Eastern

Why Middle Eastern? Because I grew up in Middle East, because there are so many amazing Middle Eastern restaurants in California, because I love playing with their spices, eggplant, hummus, labneh etc…... Here is my modest attempt to cover some of the dishes I fell in love with. It is more than just hummus.

Moroccan Harira

My husband and I ate this almost daily while we were vacationing in historical, quaint, magical, heart-warming, and breath-taking Fes in Morocco. Harira is served in small cafes, road-side eateries, hole-in-wall shops and in fancy restaurants alike. Traditionally, Harira is not vegetarian but some places do make a vegetarian version. We enjoyed it almost daily with local bread that they call crepes that were nothing like French crepes but more like Indian oiled flat bread called lacha paratha. The hospitality of people of Fes is unmatched. No matter where we ate, someone always ran to another café to fetch us vegetarian food even if they did not serve anything vegetarian. One of our favorite hole-in-wall cafes was run by two young brothers, who brought and served vegetarian food from other restaurants, all this while happily singing us Indian Bollywood hit numbers (yes, they love Bollywood movies). Did I mention magical and heart-warming Fes?

A traditional Moroccan Harira takes many hours to prepare. The recipe below is NOT a traditional Moroccan recipe. I have altered the recipe to a healthier version and to minimize cooking time and process. Who has half a day just to make a Harira, seriously? This recipe is still amazing and one of our favorites. It warms my heart and soul every time I eat it. One day, maybe we will visit Fes again. Until then, we have harira. I personally assure you will fall I love with this soup like we have.

-Vata. +Pitta. =Kapha

1 large red onion chopped

6-7 juicy Roma tomatoes pureed

½ cup French green lentils (Masoor in Hindi)

1 cup boiled garbanzo beans

1 bunch cilantro chopped coarsely (save some aside for garnish)

1 bunch Italian parsley chopped coarsely (save some aside for garnish)

1 cup uncooked noodles of your choice (traditionally wheat noodles are used but I usually use brown rice noodles)

3-4 cloves garlic minced

1 inch ginger minced

¼ -½ minced Thai or Indian green chili to taste

½ teaspoon turmeric powder

2 teaspoon cumin powder

¼ teaspoon cinnamon powder

1 pinch clove powder

4-5 Indian cinnamon sticks

Oil of your choice (that has high smoke-point)

Salt to taste

Freshly grounded black pepper to taste

Lemon or lime

3 cups water

- Wash lentils. Soak lentils in 4 cups of water for 2 hours. Boil lentils until they are soft (add more water if needed).

- In a deep stew or soup pot, heat 3-4 tablespoons of oil.

- Add whole cinnamon sticks and wait until fragrant.

- Add garlic, ginger, green chili and sauté quickly. Within few seconds, add onions.

- Sautee onions until they are light brown.

- Add powder spices and sauté in oil for about a minute (can add more oil if needed).

- Add boiled lentils, tomato puree, salt and 3 cups water and cook for 30 minutes.

- Add cilantro, parsley, noodles and cook until noodles are soft, approx 12-20 minutes (time will vary depending on type of noodles you use).

- Keep stirring and don't let noodles stick to the bottom of pan. (can add more water now).

- When noodles are almost done, add boiled garbanzo beans. Cook until noodles are soft.

- Ladle soup in soup bowls. Mix in good amount of cilantro and parsley in each bowl and freshly grounded black pepper.

- Serve with lemon or lime.

Serves 4

Middle Eastern Green Lentils soup

-Vata. +Pitta. -Kapha

1 ½ cups French Green lentils (brown Masoor)

1 large red onion chopped

4-5 juicy Roma tomatoes chopped

2 cups carrots sliced

1 cup golden potatoes peeled and cubed (optional)

3 cups (packed) spinach leaves washed and coarsely chopped

3-4 cloves garlic minced

1 inch ginger minced

¼ -½ minced Thai or Indian green chili to taste

2 teaspoons cumin powder

2 tablespoons cumin seeds

¼ teaspoon garam masala

Oil of your choice (that has high smoke-point)

Salt to taste

Freshly grounded black pepper to taste

Lemon or lime

½ cup cilantro chopped for garnish

- Wash lentils. Soak lentils in 6 cups of water for at least half an hour. Boil lentils until they are soft (add more water if needed).

- In a deep stew or soup pot, heat 2-3 tablespoons of oil.

- Add whole cumin seeds. Wait until they start popping and are aromatic.

- Add garlic, ginger, green chili and sauté for few seconds.

- Add onions. Sautee onions until they are light brown about 7-8 minutes.

- Add cumin powder and sauté in oil for about a minute (can add more oil if needed).

- Add boiled lentils, tomatoes, salt and mix well.

- Add carrots and potatoes (if using) and cook for 30 minutes. Keep stirring and don't let it stick to the bottom of pan. (Can add more water if needed).

- Add spinach, freshly grounded black pepper and garam masala. Cook for 5 minutes. Don't over-cook spinach.

- Adjust salt and black pepper if needed.

- Ladle soup in bowl. Mix in good amount of cilantro. Serve with lemon or lime.

Serves 6

Afghani 3 Lentils soup with Dill

-Vata. +Pitta. =Kapha.

½ cup yellow split pea lentils (channa dal in Hindi)

½ cup split green mung lentils

½ cup whole green mung lentils

1 large red onion chopped

4-5 juicy Roma tomatoes chopped or roughly pureed

2 cups (packed) dill leaves washed and coarsely chopped

1 cup boiled garbanzo beans

3-4 cloves garlic minced

1 inch ginger minced

¼ -½ minced Thai or Indian green chili to taste

2 teaspoons cumin powder

½ teaspoon coriander powder

2 tablespoons cumin seeds

1 tablespoon black mustard seeds

½ teaspoon garam masala

Oil of your choice (that has high smoke-point)

Salt to taste

Freshly grounded black pepper to taste

Lemon or lime

- Wash all lentils together. Soak all lentils in 6 cups of water for 2 hours. Boil lentils until they are soft (add more water if needed).

- In a deep stew or soup pot, heat 2-3 tablespoons of oil.

- Add whole cumin seeds and black mustard seeds. Wait until they start popping and are aromatic.

- Add garlic, ginger, green chili and sauté for few seconds.

- Add onions. Sautee onions until they are translucent, about 7-8 minutes.

- Add cumin powder and sauté in oil for about 30 seconds (can add more oil if needed).

- Add boiled lentils, tomatoes, salt and mix well. Cook for 30 minutes. Keep stirring and don't let lentils stick to the bottom of pan. (can add more water if needed).

- Add dill, freshly grounded black pepper, garam masala and garbanzo beans. Cook for 10 minutes. Stir often.

- Adjust salt and black pepper if needed.

- Ladle soup in bowl. Serve with lemon or lime. (Don't miss out on lemon or lime, it is important).

Serves 6

Arabian Moussaka

It is very different from Greek version and is way less time-consuming.

+Vata. ++Pitta. −Kapha

1 15-oz can garbanzo beans

1 lb Japanese or Chinese eggplant (or American eggplant in case you can't find those)

2 yellow onions chopped length-wise

3-4 ripe Roma tomatoes chopped

4 cloves garlic thinly sliced

1 cup chopped Italian parsley

Oil of your choice

Freshly ground black pepper to taste

Lime juice to taste

Salt to taste

- Take off the eggplants top. Cut them in halves length-wise.

- Turn oven to broil. Oil a baking sheet and spread eggplants. Broil them for 20 minutes turning every 5 minutes or so.

Make sure eggplant skin does not char. Let it cool.

- Heat about 6 tablespoons oil in a large pan on low heat. Add garlic to the pan and sauté for about 1-2 minutes.

- Add onions and sauté very slowly until onions are caramelized, turning constantly.

- When eggplant is cool enough to handle, separate into small chunks with a fork and mash it roughly.

- Add eggplant, garbanzo beans, tomatoes and salt to the pan and mix well.

- Cook on low heat for about 20 minutes.

- Close heat. Mix in lemon juice, black pepper, parsley and mix well.

- Serve with pita, lavash or any other flat bread.

Serves 2

Kashkeh Bademjan (Iranian Eggplant)

=Vata. +Pitta. =Kapha

1 lb Japanese or Chinese eggplant (or American eggplant in case you can't find those)

1 large yellow onion chopped length-wise

4 cloves garlic, thinly sliced

¼ cup Kashk (available at Middle Eastern grocery stores). I usually use plain full-cream yogurt or Greek yogurt instead.

¼ teaspoon cumin powder

 Any oil of your choice

3 tablespoons lime or lemon juice

Salt to taste

Freshly ground black Pepper to taste

Garnish:

1 teaspoon dry mint

½ cup chopped walnuts (optional)

Fried onions (optional)

(Original dish is garnished with small pieces of walnuts and fried onions but I don't add either of those).

- Take off the eggplants top. Cut them in halves length-wise.

- Turn oven to broil. Oil a baking sheet and spread eggplants. Broil them for 20 minutes turning every 5 minutes or so. Make sure eggplant skin does not char. Let it cool.

- Heat about 6 tablespoons oil in a large pan on low heat. Add garlic to the pan and sauté for about 1-2 minutes.

- Add onions and sauté very slowly until onions are caramelized, turning constantly.

- While onions are cooking and eggplant is cool enough to handle, mash it very lightly with a fork.

- Add cumin powder to onions and sauté for few seconds.

- Add eggplant and salt to the pan and mix well. Cook on low heat for about 5 minutes.

- Close heat. Mix in lemon juice and black pepper.

- Spread it on a shallow serving dish. Then spread Kashk or plain Greek yogurt over it.

- In a small frying pan, heat about 1 tablespoon oil. Add 2 teaspoon of dry mint leaves and fry it for 1-2 minutes

- Spread the fried mint leaves over eggplant as a garnish.

- Serve with pita, lavash or any other flat bread.

Serves 2

Middle Eastern Summer Salad with cooling greens

Traditionally, this dish is made with feta cheese. Adding dairy to this dish is against Ayuvedic food combining principles and should be avoided.

+Vata. -Pitta. +Kapha

5 scallions, thinly sliced

1 pound juicy red tomatoes or cherry tomatoes ½" diced

1 cucumber ½"diced

1 15-oz can garbanzo beans, rinsed

1/3 cup fresh parsley chopped

1/3 cup fresh mint leaves chopped

1/3 cup fresh basil leaves julienned (optional)

1/3 cup lime juice

Himalayan pink salt to taste

Freshly ground black pepper to taste

2-3 tablespoon olive oil

½ teaspoon Sumac powder

- In a large salad bowl, toss together scallions, tomatoes, cucumber, garbanzo, mint, and basil.
- In a small bowl, whisk together lime juice, salt, pepper, olive oil and Sumac.
- Pour the dressing over the salad, tossing gently to coat all the vegetables.

Serves 4

Arabic Tea

Each Middle Eastern country has its own traditional tea recipe. Yemini and Qatari tea is served with milk. Richer Middle Eastern countries add different combinations of cinnamon, green cardamom, rose water, saffron etc to their black tea and always a good dose of sugar.

Teas differ in African Arabian countries. Moroccan mint tea is actually made with green tea, fresh mint leaves and sugar. Some countries even add sage leaves.

Arabic tea is traditionally enjoyed with cubes of white sugar and served in tiny glass cups.

+Vata. =Pitta. -Kapha

1½ cup water

2 green cardamom seeded or 1/8 teaspoon freshly-grounded green cardamom powder

Few strands of saffron

Few drops of rose water

1 teaspoon loose black Ceylon tea

Sweetener of your choice (optional)

- Boil water. Add loose tea and cardamom in water.

- Close the heat, lid and let it steep for 5-6 minutes.

- Dissolve saffron in few tablespoons of rose water.

- Strain the tea in cup and add the rose-saffron water.

- Add your choice of sweetener if you like sweet taste.

Serves 1

Sweet Stuff

I know for sure you will not love me if I did not add any desserts...

Vegan Raw Almonds and Date Balls

+Vata. -Pitta. ++Kapha

1 cup almonds

½ cup dates

½ cup orange juice (can use water instead)

1 teaspoon freshly grounded green cardamom powder

2 tablespoons rose water

Coconut flakes for rolling

Unsweetened cocoa powder for rolling

- In a food processor, grind almonds to consistency of rough powder but not of flour. Remove in a large bowl.

- Add green cardamom powder to the bowl and mix well.

- Remove pits from dates.

- In the food processor, place orange juice, rose water and then dates. Blend until it is a smooth paste.

- Add date paste to the bowl and mix everything well with hands or a wooden spatula.

- Wash and dry hands. Oil your palms with little ghee and roll mixture into balls.

- Roll some balls in coconut flakes and some in cocoa powder.

- Refrigerate for 2 hours.

Kheer (Indian Rice Pudding)

This dessert can be served cold or hot, depending on the season.

-Vata. -Pitta. ++Kapha

1 cup white Basmati rice

3 cups organic full-cream or regular milk (1%, 2% or fat-free milk do not give same flavor)

2-3 tablespoons brown sugar to taste (replace with maple syrup to taste)

10 green cardamom (seeds removed, pods discarded)

1/6 cup unsalted almonds silvered or slices

1/6 cup unsalted pistachios halved or pieces

¼ cup raisins

¼ cup unsalted pistachios powdered (for garnish)

- Wash Basmati rice.

- In a sauce pan, mix 2½ cups milk, rice and sugar. On low heat, bring it to boil, stirring constantly.

- Keep stirring constantly until all milk is evaporated and rice is fully cooked.

- Keep cooking the rice while stirring it constantly until it turns into cream-colored heavy pudding like texture. This slow cooking process will give rice/milk the pudding texture and creamy taste, so do not rush.

- Now add remaining ½ cup milk, raisins, nuts and mix very well. Close heat.

- Place in serving bowls. Sprinkle generously with pistachio powder. Serve it hot.

- If serving cold: Do not add raisins. Refrigerate. Add raisins at the time of serving and mix. Sprinkle generously with pistachio powder.

Serves 4

Suji ka Halwa (Semolina Halwa)

Not only suji ka halwa is a famous house-hold dessert in sub-continent, it is also used as a prasad (sacred offering) in Hindu and Sikh temples all over south-east Asia. Also known as sheera.

-Vata. +Pitta. ++Kapha

1 cup semolina

¾ - 1 cup brown sugar to taste (replace with maple syrup to taste)

½ cup melted ghee

2 cups boiling water

¼ cup unsalted sliced almonds

¼ cup raisins

7-8 green cardamom seeds

Few strands of saffron soaked in 2 Tablespoons of water (optional)

- In a wide mouth frying pan, melt ghee on low heat.

- Add green cardamom seeds. Cook for about 1 minute until they are fragrant.

- Add semolina and roast for few minutes on low heat, constantly turning and moving it around.

- Once semolina gets one shade darker, add boiling water slowly to prevent forming lumps while stirring it constantly.

- Add sugar and dissolve it. Mix everything well so you get a smooth paste-like consistency.

- Cook it on low heat stirring constantly. When water is evaporated and semolina does not stick to the sides of the pan, halwa is done (do not rush, it will be a while).

- Mix in nuts, raisins and saffron. Serve hot.

Serves 6

Badam Halwa (Almond Halwa)

This is my husband's favorite dessert. Goji berries are not added traditionally, however, flavor of goji berries and saffron make this halwa almost sinful.

Great for students, for post-partum women, for building ojas and nourishing brain.

-Vata. +Pitta. ++Kapha

2 cups almond flour

5-6 tablespoons brown sugar to taste (can replace with maple syrup to taste)

½ cup melted ghee

¾ cup water

¼ cup goji berries

7-8 green cardamom seeds

Few strands of saffron soaked in 2 tablespoons of water (optional)

- In a wide mouth frying pan, roast almond flour on low heat, constantly turning it. Do not leave it unattended. Almond flour is roasted when it is a shade darker. Remove in a glass bowl.

- In same frying pan, melt ghee on low heat.

- Add green cardamom seeds. Cook for about 1 minute until they are fragrant.

- Add almond flour, then water and then sugar.

- Mix everything well so you get a smooth paste-like consistency.

- Mix in goji berries and saffron.

- Cook it on very low heat stirring constantly. Do not leave it unattended. When water is evaporated and halwa gets darker, and flour does not stick to the sides of the pan, halwa is done (do not rush).

Serves 6

Raw Vegan Stuffed Dates

+Vata. -Pitta. ++Kapha

1 lb large Medjool dates

½ lb pistachios meat

½ teaspoon freshly grounded green cardamom powder

1/3 cup rose water

- In a dry chopper, powder pistachio meat.

- Mix in green cardamom powder.

- Mix rose water so it is a smooth yet thick paste.

- Make a slit in dates and remove pits.

- With a small spoon, fill in the space with pistachio mix.

- Can be served cold or at room temperature. Refrigerate for an hour if serving cold.

Try other variations:

- For a more western taste: Instead of using rose water and green cardamom, use juice

of 1 medium Valencia Orange and orange peel.
- Roll finished dates in coconut powder
- Roll in dry roasted fennel seeds for an Indian taste.

"Ayurveda teaches us to cherish our innate-nature, i.e., *"to love and honor who we are"* - not as what people think or tell us, "who we should be."

~PranaJiAcupuncture.com

CPSIA information can be obtained
at www.ICGtesting.com
Printed in the USA
BVOW03s0738190217
476583BV00001B/229/P